THE ART OF PROBLEM FINDING

THE ART OF PROBLEM FINDING

Discovering the Unknown Knowns &
Unknown Unknowns

Authored By,
VASUDEVAN KIDAMBI

Disclaimer

Registered Office- 907-Sneh Nagar, Sapna Sangeeta Road,
Agrasen Square, Indore – 452001 (M.P.), India

Website: http://www.wingspublication.com

Email: mybook@wingspublication.com

First Published by WINGS PUBLICATION 2024

Title : THE ART OF PROBLEM FINDING

Price : ₹ 1,150 | $ 40 | AED 95

ISBN : 978-93-6006-848-6

LIMITS OF LIABILITY/DISCLAIMER OF WARRANTY

First Edition: 2024

Disclaimer

Dedicated To

"Dedicated to the relentless seekers of truth, the audacious challengers of convention, and the fearless explorers of possibility. May this book serve as a beacon of inspiration on your journey of problem finding, guiding you to new insights, solutions, and heights of success.

Review Request

Thank you for buying and reading my book! If you enjoyed this book and found it useful, I would be very grateful if you would post a short review online and share it on your social media with the tags #artofproblemfinding and #vasudevankidambi

About the Book

"The Art of Problem Finding - Discovering the Unknown Knowns & Unknown Unknowns" is the book that will serve its readers as a beacon for navigating the business world with innovation and strategic decision-making.

Against the dynamic backdrop of the World Economic Forum's insights into the shifting skill sets that are required in the age of AI, this groundbreaking book pioneers a departure from the conventional path of problem-solving to explore the fertile grounds of problem finding. It is here, in the identification of unseen and unasked questions, the seeds of revolutionary innovations and strategies are sown.

Historically, problem-solving has been the linchpin of progress since the dawn of the Industrial Revolution. However, the emergence of AI and advanced technologies has sparked a significant paradigm shift, compelling us to shift our focus from merely addressing existing challenges to proactively identifying and understanding new ones.

This evolution underscores the book's core belief: in an age where AI reshapes every facet of our lives, the real goldmine lies not in solving known problems but in uncovering the unknown.

Through an extensive array of real-world examples and detailed case studies, the book demonstrates the indispensable role of problem finding across diverse sectors such as technology, real estate, facilities management, gold & jewellery, automotive, and more.

It not only showcases how this approach has led to groundbreaking innovations but also equips readers with a comprehensive set of frameworks and tools to cultivate a problem-finding mindset.

Central to the book's narrative is the exploration of essential skills necessary for thriving in this new terrain such as critical thinking, curiosity, adaptability, cognitive flexibility, etc.

By fostering these skills, "The Art of Problem Finding" empowers its readers not just adapt to changes but also to lead the charge in the Brave New World of business and technology.

Further, this book delves into the psychological aspects underpinning problem finding. It sheds light on cognitive biases such as confirmation bias, anchoring bias, and status quo bias, which often impede our ability to identify latent challenges. By offering techniques to overcome these mental hurdles, the book encourages readers to embrace a more open-minded approach to discovery.

Illustrations of successful problem-finding initiatives, from Airbnb's disruption of the hospitality industry to Tesla's electrification of transportation, underscore the transformative power of looking beyond conventional solutions. These narratives serve as a testament to the book's premise that the future belongs to those who can identify and capitalize on the opportunities hidden in plain sight.

As we stand on the precipice of a new era shaped by AI, this inspirational work offers a roadmap for navigating the unknown with confidence and creativity. It challenges readers to go beyond the familiar, to question the unasked, and to uncover the opportunities that lie just beyond the horizon.

For business leaders, innovators, and curious minds alike, this book is an essential guide to leading in an unpredictable world, where the art of problem finding is the most valuable skill of all.

About the Author

Vasudevan Kidambi, widely recognized as the "LAST-MILE MAN" in the business realm, is a seasoned professional who harmonizes analytical prowess with a human-centric approach to problem-solving. With over three decades of experience, he has emerged as a pivotal figure in corporate operations and consultancy, earning the trust of elite organizations and executives. Vasudevan's journey into the depths of Generative AI and his advocacy for One-Page Communication underscore his innovative spirit and commitment to enhancing corporate communications.

As the Managing Director of Navo Informatica Pvt. Ltd and Navo Management Consultants, Vasudevan has spearheaded the integration of AI into strategic business frameworks, pioneering AI-enabled content development. His expertise extends to AI tools application in business consulting, change management, and growth marketing, transforming digital and content strategies across global enterprises.

With a keen eye for details, Vasudevan has long championed the shift from problem-solving to problem finding, a skill recently highlighted by the World Economic Forum as crucial for leadership. His approach, rooted in curiosity-driven critical thinking, has been a cornerstone of his consulting services for over a decade, fostering digital transformations and benefiting many multinational corporations.

An esteemed educator and AI thought leader, Vasudevan's commitment to demystifying AI for professionals through boot camps and webinars exemplifies his dedication to empowering businesses in the digital age. His forthcoming book reflects a culmination of years of pioneering problem-finding exercises, positioning Vasudevan as a visionary in the ever-evolving corporate landscape.

He had developed and included a groundbreaking framework - Kidambi's Data-Driven Problem Finding Framework - in this book which challenges the conventional thinking of problem finding. It emphasizes the importance of changing the question to uncover hidden insights and opportunities.

To learn more about his multifaceted career and contributions, contact him through,

Email: Vasudevan.K@navoinc.com

Link-in-bio: www.linktr.ee/vasudevankidambi

Foreword

In the ever-evolving landscape of business and technology, where change is not just constant but accelerating, the ability to solve problems has long been hailed as a cornerstone of success. However, as we find ourselves propelled into the age of artificial intelligence and unprecedented technological advancement, the very nature of problem-solving is undergoing a profound transformation.

It is within this context of rapid change and complexity that Vasudevan's "The Art of Problem Finding - Discovering the Unknown Knowns & Unknown Unknowns" emerges as a beacon of guidance and enlightenment.

Vasudevan who I lovingly call Vasu brings to the forefront a wealth of experience and insight garnered over three decades of navigating the intricacies of corporate operations and consultancy. His unique blend of analytical prowess and human-centric approach has earned him the trust of elite organizations and executives, making him a pivotal figure in the field of problem finding.

At its core, this book challenges us to transcend the conventional paradigms of problem-solving and venture into the uncharted territories of problem finding. In a world where the pace of change outstrips our ability to keep up, the book reminds us that the real source of innovation and strategic advantage lies not in addressing known challenges but in uncovering the unknown.

Drawing from a diverse array of real-world examples and detailed case studies spanning various sectors, Vasudevan Kidambi meticulously illustrates the transformative potential of problem finding. From the tech industry to real estate, from facilities management to automotive, the book showcases how this shift in perspective has sparked revolutionary innovations and reshaped entire industries.

In essence, I found this publication to be more than just a book; it is a blueprint for the future of innovation. It calls upon us to embrace uncertainty, to interrogate our assumptions, and to embark on a voyage of discovery where the art of problem finding reigns supreme.

As we stand on the cusp of a new era shaped by AI and technological disruption, let us heed the wisdom contained within these pages and embrace the art of problem finding as the most invaluable skill of all.

Prof Jeevan D'Mello

GDArch, CMCA, AMS, LSM, PCAM, D. Litt

President, Community Associations Institute, USA

President, Global Leaders Today, USA

CEO, Zenesis Corporation, UAE

Professor of Practice, Woxsen University, India

Former Board Member, Rotary Club of Dubai, UAE

Foreword

As I reflect on my journey of innovation and disruption, I am humbled and honoured to lend my voice to Vasudevan Kidambi's ground-breaking book, "The Art of Problem Finding - Discovering the Unknown Knowns and Unknown Unknowns." In a world where conformity often reigns supreme, Kidambi champions a different approach—one that celebrates curiosity, challenges the status quo, and embraces the unknown.

Throughout my career, I have been driven by a relentless desire to push boundaries and redefine what is possible. From envisioning circular Target sports and games to disrupting the Arabic fonts to different styles, I have always sought to challenge conventional thinking and spark innovation. It is this same spirit of exploration and discovery that resonates deeply with Kidambi's work.

In "The Art of Problem Finding," Kidambi invites readers to embark on a journey of exploration, encouraging them to look beyond the surface and uncover hidden opportunities. Drawing on his own experiences and insights, he offers practical strategies and tools for cultivating a curiosity-led mindset and navigating the complexities of problem finding.

As a visionary leader, Kidambi has not only reshaped the way we approach problem finding but also the way we communicate. What sets Kidambi apart is his unwavering commitment to questioning everything and his ability to see potential where others see obstacles.

In "The Art of Problem Finding," Kidambi shares his insights, wisdom, and passion for problem finding with the world, inspiring readers to embrace curiosity, challenge the status quo, and unlock the hidden potential within themselves and their organizations. It is my sincere hope that this book will empower readers to become fearless innovators and problem finders, charting a course toward a brighter and more innovative future.

Moreover, Kidambi's approach aligns with the World Economic Forum's call for a shift from Problem Solving Skills to Problem Finding Skills. With the advent of AI taking over routine problem-solving tasks, cultivating problem-finding skills becomes paramount for future leaders to stay ahead in an ever-evolving landscape.

Ghanim Al Falasi

Senior Vice President of Technology Ecosystem and Development

Dubai Silicon Oasis, DIEZ, UAE

Foreword

Long before this book gets to a few reprints, we may be ushering in Artificial General Intelligence (AGI) into our lives. As someone who spent majority of Mac career in AI industry, I keep getting questioned from both students and industry on what happens to human jobs in the future and if indeed development of products are being taken over by AI including (& not limited to) coding, testing, debugging etc, what remains for humans to do.

Well, amidst this whirlwind of AI technological progress shaping our lives, "The Art of Problem Finding" emerges as a beacon, guiding us through the labyrinth of innovation and strategic foresight.

Departing from the traditional problem-solving approach, this ground-breaking book champions the practice of problem finding, where the true gems of innovation and business opportunity lies.

The narrative begins by tracing the historical evolution from problem-solving, a cornerstone of progress since the Industrial Revolution, to the imperative of problem finding in today's AI-driven landscape. Through meticulous exploration and real-world examples spanning diverse sectors, the book underscores the indispensable art of problem finding in uncovering hidden opportunities and shaping the future. Central to the book's ethos is the cultivation of essential skills like critical thinking and adaptability.

Delving into the psychology of problem finding, the book addresses cognitive biases that often hinder our ability to identify latent challenges.

It advocates for an open-minded approach, encouraging readers to embrace curiosity and explore beyond conventional solutions.

Through compelling case studies, from Airbnb's disruption of hospitality to Tesla's electrification of transportation, the book reemphasised that the future belongs to those who can uncover opportunities hidden in plain sight.

In conclusion, "The Art of Problem Finding" is more than a book; it's a manifesto for the future of innovation. As we navigate the complexities of the AI era, this book heralds problem finding as the most valuable skill in an unpredictable world. As I close my foreword and appreciation of Vasu's book, remember where we started - what do humans do if AI does everything - well consumption, structures, governance of AI, fine-tuned products, nuanced platforms with the help of AI say a personalised movie for yourself, an ad stream that's totally based on your needs latent and may be relevant , security needs for humans etc there a plethora of opportunities for us to find - yes problem finding is the key !

SATISH MEDAPATI

Chief Data Officer

Movius Interactive Corporation, USA

Patent (Few) holder in AL / ML, Top 20 influential conversational AI leaders of India (2021), NASSCOM Foundation Council Member (2022), Amazon AI Conclave – ML Elevate 2021 Winner.

Acknowledgement

I would like to express my deepest gratitude to all those who have contributed to the realization of this book. Your support, encouragement, and expertise have been invaluable throughout this journey.

First and foremost, I extend my heartfelt thanks to Ms. Ramadevi for her tireless efforts in ensuring the quality and integrity of this document. Her attention to detail has greatly enriched the final product.

Special thanks to Lakshmi Ratan for his invaluable guidance on key concepts and his valuable feedback on the content, which greatly enhanced clarity and precision to this work.

I am also immensely grateful to my industry colleagues and well-wishers who generously responded to my request for advance praise. Your feedback and encouragement have been instrumental in shaping this book.

Special thanks are due to Jeevan D Mello, Ghanim Al Falasi, and Satish Medapati for their insightful forewords, which have added depth and perspective to the narrative.

I would be remiss if I did not acknowledge the unwavering support of my family. To my wife, Anuradha, and my son, Aneesh Kidambi, thank you for your patience, understanding, and unwavering belief in me.

I am also indebted to Dr. Kailash Pinjani and Dr. Deepak Parbat for their guidance and support throughout this endeavour. Your wisdom and expertise have been invaluable in shaping the direction of this book.

Finally, I extend my heartfelt thanks to all those whose names may not appear here but whose contributions have been equally significant. Your support has made this journey possible, and I am truly grateful.

Thank you all for being an integral part of "THE ART OF PROBLEM FINDING - Discovering the Unknown Knowns & Unknown Unknowns."

With sincere appreciation,

Vasudevan Kidambi

Testimonials

"In the evolving landscape of AI-driven innovation, 'The Art of Problem Finding: Discovering the Unknown Knowns & Unknown Unknowns' by Vasudevan Kidambi offers a transformative perspective. As I know Vasu for his remarkable ability to translate his extensive experience and knowledge into simple yet powerful solutions for even the most complex issues, this book embodies that very strength. With practical insights and tools, the book advocates for a paradigm shift in problem-solving, emphasizing the importance of recognizing unknown challenges as catalysts for innovation. This essential guide equips readers with skills for success in today's dynamic environment, empowering them to uncover hidden opportunities and navigate uncharted waters."

- Ayed Alqahtani, Senior Director,
Asset Transition, KAFD, Saudi Arabia

The Art of Problem Finding" is for anyone looking to thrive in the AI-driven innovation era. It offers practical frameworks and tools to cultivate a problem-finding mindset, essential for identifying unseen challenges. With real-world examples and expert insights, this book equips business leaders with the skills to navigate a rapidly evolving landscape and turn hidden challenges into opportunities for growth. It is a roadmap for “futureproofing” in today's dynamic business environment.

– C.V. Nagarajan, CEO, Dutco Tennant LLC, UAE

"A masterful blend of theory and practice, 'The Art of Problem Finding' by Vasudevan Kidambi empowers leaders and innovators. With profound wisdom and actionable strategies, it guides readers to anticipate change, uncover opportunities, and drive growth in today's fast-paced world."

- Ashish Kapahi, CEO, GATES APAC, Singapore

“Explore the intricacies of problem finding, innovation, and curiosity in this enlightening book. Discover how fostering a culture of learning and leveraging interdisciplinary insights can lead to groundbreaking solutions and a brighter future. A must -read for those passionate about pushing boundaries and driving progress.”

- Kamran Birjees Khan, CEO, Nia Ltd, UAE

"In 'The Art of Problem Finding,' Vasu urges a shift to proactive problem-finding, offering rich insights and strategies for navigating today's complexities. It's more than a guide; it's a manifesto for fostering curiosity, innovation, and resilience. Essential for leaders and innovators."

- Suresh G, CEO, CGVAK Software (USA) Inc., USA

"When pitching a product, the question 'What problem are you solving?' is paramount. Vasu's book illuminates the evolving landscape and with his insightful guidance, the book equips entrepreneurs with the skills to anticipate and prepare for the unknown. It is refreshingly simple and digestible; yet precise and deep. Highly recommended for upcoming founders, young entrepreneurs, and innovators.

- Parthasarathy, Chairman, CADD Centre Group, India

"The Art of Problem Finding - Discovering the Unknown Knowns & Unknown Unknowns" is a compelling resource for corporate executives seeking sustainable growth. Whether navigating startups or established enterprises, anticipating future challenges is key. While Black Swans are unpredictable, proactive scenario planning is vital. This book offers a disciplined approach to identifying potential issues on the horizon, ensuring readiness for whatever the future holds.

-Raj Shankar, Ex-Vice Chairman and MD of Redington Limited, Singapore

Vasu reminds me of the medical surgeons. Deep and critical exploration of significantly agile business circumstances consequentially resulting in a "go to" exclusive bible for entrepreneurs and management personnel. Only Vasu can do this with his dedication, perseverance, and passion. The Art of Problem Finding - Discovering the Unknown Knowns & Unknown Unknowns is one such rendition so efficiently curated on the evolutionary AI – a must for today's corporate world. My best wishes to Vasu for authoring more and more useful books like this.

-Geethalakshmi Ramachandran, Managing Counsel, ABA Legal Consultants, UAE

You may have a solution mindset but if you identify the wrong problem, you and your team could be barking up the wrong tree for a long time. The Art of Problem finding is a timely book written by Vasudevan Kidambi who I have known to be a thinker and analyser par excellence. With this book Vasu lays out a roadmap to find the right problems and communicate then correctly to all stakeholders before embarking on solution finding. A must read.

- Sandhya Prakash, Thought Leader, TEDx Speaker, Author and Advisor, Wissen Technology, India

"After many years of business problem solving Mr. Kidambi is bringing to us a valuable series of books from communication to corporate confusion and now to problem finding. With his rich experience he takes us in a clear simplest way to tackle the unknown business world. Outstanding achievement."

– Dikran Tchablakian, CEO, TecBuy, UAE

"In 'The Art of Problem Finding,' Vasu expertly illuminates the path to uncovering hidden challenges in our ever-evolving world. With a compelling blend of knowledge and real-life examples, this book serves as a beacon for those navigating the AI-driven era. It not only underscores the importance of identifying problems but also provides readers with the tools to do so effectively. A must-read for innovators and leaders navigating future complexities."

– Ozgur Baslilar, Commercial & Operations Lead & Board Member, Kenvue, UAE

In his new book, Vasu has seemingly built a dictionary for the corporate buzz language. To conceptually think an idea of this nature in the form of a book itself is laudable, and then to explore it to its depths the way he has done is commendable. I think it's a must-read for everyone across the corporate ladder so that these words sometimes loosely used get both context and meaning.

– Rahul Nagpal, Chairman & CEO, GP Inc, UAE

"In 'The Art of Problem Finding,' Vasudevan Kidambi offers invaluable guidance for leaders navigating uncertainty and driving innovation. With insightful frameworks and real-world examples, this book equips Business School students with the tools needed to thrive in today's rapidly changing business landscape. As Dean, I commend Kidambi for delivering a pioneering guide that empowers everyone to uncover hidden opportunities and drive strategic growth with confidence. I am of a solid opinion that this book is a must-read for aspiring business leaders."

– Dr. J. Clement Sudhahar, Ph.D.., Dean, Karunya School of Management, India

"The book explores the paradigm shift from problem-solving to problem-finding in the age of AI and advanced technologies. It argues that the future of innovation and strategic decision-making lies in identifying and understanding new challenges, rather than merely addressing existing ones!

Nicely narrated by a seasoned and experienced leader in Vasu"

- Narayanan, KV, Channel Head - Middle East & Africa at HP Inc., UAE

I've had the privilege of collaborating with Vasudevan Kidambi for many years, and I can attest to the transformative impact of his problem-finding skills and unwavering commitment to challenging the status quo. His pioneering work in identifying unknown knowns has been invaluable to many organizations.

Both in his consulting services and now in his book, 'The Art of Problem Finding,' Vasudevan Kidambi continues to empower the business community with actionable insights and innovative strategies. I've personally benefited greatly from his expertise, and I highly recommend this book to anyone looking to navigate uncertainty and drive meaningful change in their organization."

– Santosh Vargheese, Vice President, Toshiba Gulf FZE, UAE

"In this new boundless world where creativity meets technology, Vasudevan K.S. emerges as a new age visionary, illuminating paths yet untraveled. With words as his compass and AI as his guide, he pioneers a new era of problem finding and solving, reshaping the landscape of innovation. With the adept touch of a business guru and the innovative spirit of a visionary, he unveils the limitless possibilities of generative AI, forging a future where imagination knows no bounds."

- Carl Castellino, General Manager, Al Mirqab Group, Qatar

The Art of Problem Finding - Discovering the Unknown Knowns & Unknown Unknowns" is a transformative guide that resonates deeply. Authored with clarity and insight, it illuminates the crucial shift towards problem finding in an AI-driven world. As CEO, I highly recommend this book to business leaders and innovators seeking to navigate complex landscapes with foresight and agility. It's an indispensable resource for turning challenges into opportunities for growth.

- Abraham Kah, CEO, Mai Dubai Water, UAE

"As someone who has had the pleasure of witnessing Vasudevan Kidambi's professionalism and articulation firsthand, I can confidently say that 'The Art of Problem Finding' is a testament to his exceptional storytelling abilities. Through insightful narratives and practical wisdom, Kidambi invites readers on a journey of discovery, challenging them to think differently and embrace curiosity. His unique approach to problem finding is both refreshing and enlightening, making this book a must-read for anyone seeking to unlock their creative potential and drive innovation."

- Yasser Tufail, VP-Operations, Technical Centre of Excellence, KAFD, Saudi Arabia

"Vasu is a powerful storyteller, always bringing rich colour to the black and white world of data analytics. With this book, he puts people back at the centre of the problem handling process - encouraging business leaders and innovators to hunt for problems as a means to unlock new opportunities."

- Ryan Mackey, Director GATES Summits, Singapore

Vasudevan Kidambi rightly deserves commendation for restructuring the problem-solving sequence. To solve, one must identify the core issue or dissect the existing problem, as any identified problem is partly solved with additional complications. The book lucidly elucidates these dynamics, steering away from the problem to introduce the nuances of AI. Its coherence and free-flowing nature deserve praise, as it avoids circuitous detours and offers readers a different perspective. Upon perusal, I found a detailed yet distinct presentation, justifying its emergence and presence.!

- Prof. R. Venkatapathy, Ph.D. B.L. FDPM (IIM-A), Associate Dean Faculty of Management MMU - Malaysia (2007-8), Director BSMED (1999 - 2016) & Dean, Bharathiar University, India

A must-read for leaders navigating today's unpredictable terrain, 'The Art of Problem Finding' by Vasudevan is a pioneering work blending practical wisdom and real-world examples. It guides readers to uncover hidden gems amidst uncertainty, celebrating curiosity, foresight, and adaptability. Vasudevan empowers readers to embrace change and drive innovation with visionary insights and actionable strategies, poised to become a cornerstone for thriving amidst complexity.

- Shabana Shah, CEO, Trident Consulting Inc, USA

In a world of uncertainty, accurately identifying and solving complex problems is essential for sustainable business growth. This book serves as a valuable guide for entrepreneurs, students, and professionals, offering insights to navigate uncertainty and drive success through agility and forward-thinking mindset.

- Taeho Roh, Executive Vice President, Hansol Paper Co. Ltd, South Korea

The say “If it ain’t broke, don’t fix it.” Well, as paradigm busters go, “The Art of Problem Finding” is as powerful as they come. This is a book that will explain the necessity to look well beyond what is now working in order to discover possibilities hidden to most others. It then equips you with the knowledge and tools that allow you the courage to embark on these fascinating journeys. You will be able to put the mindset of “First Mover Advantage” and, “Being “Proactive vs, Reactive” on steroids

- Nabil Skaria, Founder & MD, Outpace Consulting, Egypt

Contents

01

Introduction: The Paradigm Shift in Problem Handling

INTRODUCTION

A. The Evolution of Problem Handling

From Problem-Solving to Problem-Finding

In the last couple of decades, I have experienced a need for a significant shift in how businesses approach challenges. Traditionally, businesses were reactive, focusing on existing issues and finding solutions, approaching everything from a Root-Cause-Analysis (RCA) perspective. This approach was the heart of problem solving during the first two decades of the 21st century. However, in the modern era, marked by rapid technological advancement, coupled with unpredictability, this reactive approach is often found to be inadequate.

As I have seen, businesses are increasingly recognizing the value of problem-finding, a proactive process that involves identifying potential problems or unmet needs before they become apparent. This shift reflects a deeper understanding that *the most significant opportunities and breakthroughs often lie in uncharted territories – in questions not yet asked and problems not yet perceived.*

Industrial Revolution to AI Revolution

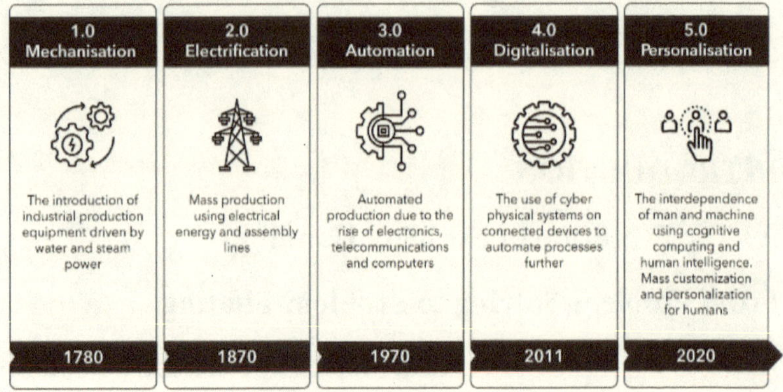

Fig 1.1: Industrial Revolution & Society 5.0

We know that the Industrial Revolution was characterized by the focus on solving known problems – how to increase production, enhance efficiency, and reduce labour costs. When we fast forward to the current scenario with AI Revolution, the focus has pivoted. It is now about leveraging technologies like artificial intelligence to anticipate challenges, identify emerging trends, and uncover hidden opportunities.

Unlike the linear and often predictable challenges of the past, today's problems are complex, multifaceted, and often interconnected. AI's ability to process vast amounts of data and identify patterns offers unprecedented opportunities for problem-finding.

I believe that having this capability allows businesses to stay ahead of the curve, adapt quickly, and innovate consistently. Look at the infographic visual below illustrating the timeline from the Industrial Revolution to the AI Revolution. It highlights the key milestones in business problem-solving approaches, *contrasting the past focus on efficiency with the current emphasis on innovation and anticipation.*

Here, I would like to point out the benefits of shifting our focus from problem solving to problem finding.

Plays a Role in Innovation and Competitive Edge

The ability to identify and address problems before they arise can provide a significant competitive advantage to businesses. Companies like Apple and Tesla have excelled not just by solving existing problems, but by identifying and addressing the needs that consumers themselves were not even aware of. *This forward-thinking approach leads to innovation, customer loyalty, and a strong market position.*

Helps in adapting to Rapid Technological Changes

In a world where technological, social, political, economic, and other situations evolve rapidly, businesses need to anticipate and adapt quickly. This requires more than just reacting to technological changes; it involves using these changes as a springboard for problem finding. I will say, businesses must continuously scan the horizon for emerging technologies, understand their potential implications, and identify the new opportunities they offer.

B. Significance of Problem Finding in Current Business Environment

It is known well that the ability to proactively identify and address newer challenges and opportunities is a significant competitive advantage.

I have understood and propose that *this essentially requires a culture of curiosity, continuous learning, and readiness to change.* Let me detail all these qualities and skill requirements in each of the oncoming chapters and list out the tools and techniques that are needed to acquire and make use of them.

Implementing a Problem-Finding Strategy

In order to adopt a problem-finding approach one should involve the following key strategies:

1. **Nurturing a Culture of Curiosity and Learning**: Encourage employees to ask questions, explore new ideas, and challenge existing assumptions. Promote continuous learning and exploration across all levels of the organization.
2. **Adopting Design Thinking and Empathetic Exploration**: Use design thinking methodologies

to deeply understand customers' unmet needs and desires. Empathetic exploration can uncover insights that data alone cannot reveal.

3. **Leveraging Inter-Disciplinary Insights**: Draw on diverse perspectives and expertise from across different fields and industries. Inter-disciplinary collaboration can spark innovative ideas and uncover hidden problems and opportunities.
4. **Encouraging Experimentation and Tolerance for Failure**: Create an environment where experimentation is encouraged, and failure is seen as a valuable learning experience. This can foster innovation and lead to unexpected discoveries.

Once we have these key strategies in place in the organization, it will be a paradigm shift towards problem finding mindset.

Conclusion: Need for the focus shift

We understood now that there is an urgent need to shift our focus from problem solving to problem finding. Instead of waiting for the problems to arise, we should be proactive in identifying the potential issues. This means looking for areas where problems might occur in the near or distant future, even if they are not obvious now. This is where this book has taken the lead and can help you gain the knowledge and information you need to tackle these hidden challenges, *both the unknown knowns and unknown unknowns.*

02

The New Frontier - Understanding Problem Finding

What is Problem Finding?

I will define it as a strategic approach that focuses on identifying new, emerging, or potential problems. It's about understanding what our customers might need before they express it, or foreseeing the market shifts before they occur. This concept in my view is central to design thinking and innovation, where the goal is to uncover the root cause of issues or the deeper needs of customers that haven't yet been addressed.

Problem finding involves a deep understanding of the context, an openness to new insights, and a willingness to question assumptions. It's about looking beyond the obvious and exploring the 'what ifs.'

Comparison with Problem-Solving

Let's dig deeper to compare it with problem solving. While problem-solving is about addressing known challenges, problem-finding is about anticipating and uncovering unknown or hidden challenges.

Problem-solving often employs a linear approach – you identify the problem, analyze it, and solve it.

Problem-finding, however, is non-linear and exploratory. It involves identifying trends, questioning existing paradigms, and looking for potential problems that could emerge.

In the next section, we will see some tools and techniques for both and how the thinking differs for them.

Tools & Techniques for Problem Finding and Problem Solving

A. Problem Finding: Involves more creative, curiosity-led and anticipatory methods.

Key tools include:

- **Connecting Silo data:** Finding new patterns, raising new questions, challenging the status quo
- **Trend Analysis**: To spot emerging patterns and potential future issues.
- **Scenario Planning**: Imagining various future scenarios to identify potential problems.
- **Ethnographic Research**: Understanding user behaviour and needs that are not yet articulated.
- **Customer Feedback Forums**: Engaging with customers to explore unexpressed needs.

B. Problem Solving: Employs structured and analytical techniques.

Most used tools are:

- **Root Cause Analysis**: To identify the underlying cause of a problem.
- **Six Sigma Methodologies**: For process improvement and quality control.
- **Decision Matrices**: To evaluate and prioritize solutions.
- **Simulation Models**: For testing potential solutions in a controlled environment.

Thinking Requirements

A. Problem Finding:

- **Level of Thinking**: Strategic and high-level.
- **Kind of Thinking**: Creative, divergent, and abstract, focusing on 'what could be'. A 'curious' and agile mindset will fast-track 'problem-finding' skillset.

B. Problem Solving:

- **Level of Thinking**: Operational and detailed.
- **Kind of Thinking**: Analytical, convergent, and logical, focusing on 'what is'. A structured, disciplined, and analytical mindset will aid 'problem-solving skillset.

Comparative Table:

I have provided a comprehensive view in the table below for understanding the distinct roles and methods of problem finding and problem solving. It will highlight the importance of both in different stages of business strategy and operations, underlining the need for a balanced approach that incorporates both creative foresight and analytical rigor.

Problem Finding vs. Problem Solving

Parameter	Problem Finding	Problem Solving
Objective	To identify new, emerging, or potential problems, often unarticulated needs, or opportunities.	To address and find solutions to known, defined problems or challenges.
Nature	Proactive, anticipatory, and exploratory.	Reactive, focused, and often linear.
Approach	Open-ended, involves questioning the status quo and challenging assumptions.	Structured, follows a systematic process to address the identified problem.

Tools & Techniques	Brainstorming, trend analysis, SWOT analysis (modified for emerging opportunities), customer feedback forums, ethnographic research, scenario planning.	Root cause analysis, Six Sigma, Pareto analysis, flowcharts, mind mapping, decision matrices, simulation models.
Type of Thinking	Divergent thinking, creative thinking, strategic foresight.	Convergent thinking, analytical thinking, logical reasoning.
Level of Thinking	High-level, involves big-picture thinking and future-oriented perspectives.	Detailed level, focused on immediate and specific aspects of a problem.
Outcome	Identification of new areas for innovation or improvement, setting the stage for future problem-solving.	Resolving or mitigating an existing issue, leading to immediate improvements or fixes.
Examples	Identifying an unmet consumer need that leads to a new product category; foreseeing a market shift due to emerging technology.	Developing a solution for a manufacturing defect; implementing a new process to improve customer service efficiency.
Required Skills	Curiosity, ability to think abstractly, being comfortable with ambiguity, having empathy and foresight.	Analytical skills, attention to detail, process-oriented thinking, technical or specific knowledge, problem-solving skills.

Conclusion – Looking beyond the obvious

It is understood that Problem finding is a crucial skill which allows businesses to anticipate and address potential problems before they occur, giving them a competitive edge. Problem finding is a strategic approach that requires a deep understanding of the context, a willingness to question assumptions, and an openness to new ideas. It is about looking beyond the obvious and exploring the "what ifs."

It is distinct from problem-solving, which is a tactical approach that focuses on addressing known challenges. By using a combination of problem-finding and problem-solving techniques, businesses can improve their ability to innovate and adapt to change.

03

Problem Finding is NOT Fault Finding

As the world of businesses continuously evolve and innovate, the concepts of problem finding, and fault finding are often misconstrued as interchangeable. However, the distinction between them is not just semantic but fundamentally different in approach and outcome.

Let me bring out their differences with clear examples.

Problem Finding: The Art of Uncovering Possibilities

Problem finding is an anticipatory, creative process that involves identifying challenges or opportunities before they become apparent. I can say that it's about looking beyond the immediate horizon, asking "what if," and exploring uncharted territories.

This proactive approach is crucial for innovation, as it allows businesses and individuals to anticipate changes, adapt strategies, and create solutions that address future needs. Problem finding is akin to a treasure hunt, where the goal is to discover the hidden gems (opportunities) rather than to spotlight the flaws.

Fault Finding: The Science of Pinpointing Errors

Contrastingly, fault finding is a reactive process focused on identifying errors or defects after they have occurred. It's about analyzing what went wrong, diagnosing issues within existing systems or products, and implementing corrective measures.

While fault finding is necessary for quality control and improvement, it does not inherently drive innovation or uncover new opportunities.

Imagine if Christopher Columbus - in his quest for new routes - was into merely fault finding, he might have ended up critiquing the compass for not pointing directly to India, rather than uncovering a whole new continent. "This compass must be broken; it's leading us into uncharted waters!" he might have complained, missing the point (and the discovery) entirely.

Or consider a chef exploring new recipes who focuses solely on fault finding: "This dish is too spicy; that one's too bland." Amidst all the critique, he/she might never stumble upon the next culinary delight. It's the difference between a chef who invents a new cuisine and the one who can't move past the salt level in the soup.

Imagine a leading technology distribution company which has long been a pioneer in the industry. The CEO, Alex, convenes a strategy meeting with the top executives to discuss the company's future direction in the fast-evolving tech landscape.

Scenario 1: Fault Finding Approach

Alex begins the meeting by highlighting the declining sales of their flagship product. The discussion quickly spirals into a fault-finding session. Departments point fingers at each other: Marketing blames Sales for not leveraging the marketing spend, while Sales criticizes Marketing for ineffective promotion and blames finance for not acting fast enough. The meeting ends with action items focused solely on fixing these "faults," but no new ideas or directions emerge. The atmosphere is tense, and morale is low.

Scenario 2: Problem Finding Approach

In an alternate scenario, Alex steers the conversation towards unmet customer needs and emerging technological

trends. Instead of focusing on what went wrong, the team explores "what if" questions: What if we could solve a problem our customers don't yet know they have? What emerging technologies can we leverage? The shift towards problem finding ignites creativity and collaboration. Ideas flow freely, leading to the conceptualization of a revolutionary new product that addresses a future market need.

The illustrations above vividly depict the outcomes of fault finding and problem finding in a business context. While the former can lead to stagnation and internal conflict, the latter fosters innovation, team cohesion, and strategic growth, guiding the company towards uncharted territories of success.

Conclusion – Exploring the unknown

Understanding the difference between problem finding and fault finding is crucial. While one focuses on identifying and rectifying errors, the other is about exploring the unknown for opportunities. Embracing problem finding is embracing the potential for growth, innovation, and discovery. So, the next time you are faced with a challenge, remember you are not just looking for what is broken—you are searching for the next breakthrough. And who knows? You might just find it in the least expected place, as long as you're not too distracted by the compass's misdirection!

04

AI and Problem Finding - A Collaborative Relationship

In the past couple of years, with the advent of ChatGPT 3.5 and with multiple AI tools taking the world by storm, it is getting more and more interesting to see their effect on various industries. With my hands on experience with generative AI technology and tools, it is understating to say that Artificial intelligence (AI) has grown to be a disruptive force in the business and technology world. AI is not just a tool for solving issues but also plays the role as a collaborator in problem discovery.

In this chapter let's explore the mutually beneficial link between artificial intelligence (AI) and problem finding, detailing how this collaboration is altering the nature of problem identification and fostering human capacity for creative thought and innovation.

Broadly, we can group the influence of AI into 4 areas:

A. Discovering hidden patterns
B. Deepening our understanding
C. Encouraging cross-disciplinary insights
D. Fostering creativity

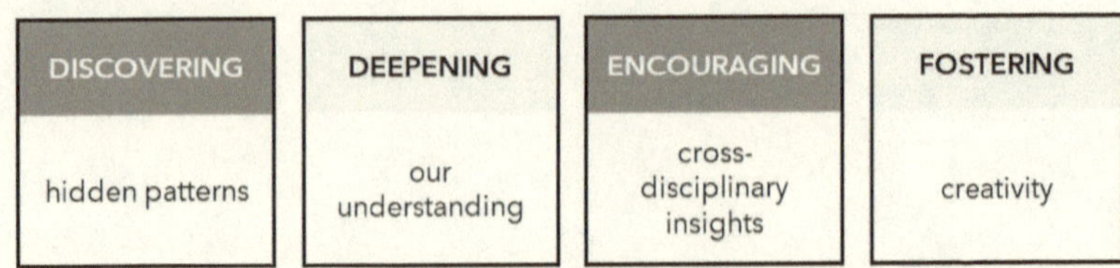

Fig 4.1: Areas of AI Influence

I provide my insights on each of these areas how AI is useful to identify the unknown issues.

A. Discovering hidden patterns

The first step in exploring the world of AI-assisted problem finding is realizing how special AI is. *Artificial intelligence (AI) systems can analyze large datasets, identify trends, and even identify areas of concern that may not be immediately apparent to human observers, in contrast to traditional problem-solving methods that rely on established parameters.*

This ability to generate insights from data offers up new possibilities for detecting possible problems before they become obvious or serious.

AI's unmatched capacity to go through data and spot trends and abnormalities that escape traditional analysis is the foundation of its contribution to problem finding.

This is especially important for companies where there is an abundance of data that is too much for humans to evaluate and understand. AI functions as a lighthouse, alerting organizations to areas that need attention or more research by emphasizing these trends.

B. Deepening our understanding

Not only can AI identify possible issues, but it also plays a critical role in filling up knowledge gaps. *AI may provide a more comprehensive understanding of the problems at hand by identifying relationships and linkages that were previously hidden by evaluating data from a variety of sources.*

C. Encouraging cross-disciplinary insights

One of AI's advantages is *its capacity to incorporate information from other disciplines, which encourages a cross-disciplinary approach to problem finding.*

Let me say that this ensures solutions are impacted by diverse perspectives, boosts their creativity and effectiveness, also improves the creative process.

D. Fostering creativity

AI's ability to analyze data is widely established, but it also has a big influence on creativity. *AI frees up human cognitive resources by taking on the labour-intensive tasks associated with data processing, enabling people and groups to focus more intently on the creative components of problem finding.*

Practically, whatever AI discovers will act as a catalyst for more research, encouraging us to pose novel queries and consider previously unthinkable scenarios. More sophisticated and forward-thinking problem identification results from this iterative conversation between human intuition and AI's data-driven recommendations.

When we propel this understanding, it takes us to the collaborative future where human and AI work together to anticipate and solve problems.

The Collaborative Future: Human-AI Collaborations for problem finding

It fascinates me to imagine the possibilities for collaborating between humans and artificial intelligence in the field of problem finding and the potential is limitless. Through this collaboration, there is a hope to redefine creativity and innovation itself, as well as improve our capacity to recognize and respond to obstacles. Needless to say, there are strengths and threats too in this partnership going further, as we see next.

Combining Strengths:

To maximize the potential of this mutually beneficial collaboration, it is essential to utilize the unique strengths that humans and AI bring to the table. *AI excels at analyzing data and identifying patterns, while humans possess a superior ability in problem-solving, empathy, and addressing ethical concerns.*

By combining these strengths, a more comprehensive and refined approach to problem finding can be achieved.

Handling Ethical Issues:

However, there are some ethical issues such as data privacy, bias, and decision-making transparency are becoming more and more crucial as AI is incorporated into problem-finding process. It is essential that we make sure AI systems are developed and used with these issues in mind if we want to build trust and keep the integrity of the problem-finding process.

Conclusion: The collaborative future ahead

The use of AI in problem-finding represents a significant advancement in our understanding of both the challenges and opportunities that lie ahead. By leveraging AI's analytical capabilities, businesses and people can discover hidden patterns and knowledge gaps that would otherwise be missed. This can lead to more creative problem-solving and the development of innovative solutions.

However, the AI revolution in problem-solving also challenges us to rethink the way we approach creativity and innovation. The human element remains essential, as it is the combination of human knowledge and AI's analytical abilities that offers the most promising path forward. By working together, we can unlock new avenues for problem finding and create solutions that are both imaginative and practical. The connection between AI and human creativity serves as a testament to our collective capacity to push the boundaries of what's possible.

05

The Hidden Depths - Recognizing Unknown Knowns & Unknown Unknowns

In an era marked by rapid technological, social, political, and economic shifts, the ability of businesses to not only anticipate but also adapt to change is more crucial than ever. In this chapter I delve into the art and science of navigating the murky waters of unknown knowns & unknown unknowns – the challenges and opportunities that *lie beyond our current understanding and anticipation.*

Drawing from a collection of corporate illustrations, expert insights, and the strategic application of analytical frameworks like PESTEL (Political Economical Social Technological Environmental & Legal), let us explore how businesses can cultivate resilience and foresight in the face of unpredictability.

Understanding Unknown Knowns & Unknown Unknowns: Exploring what we don't know

The term " unknown knowns & unknown unknowns" gained prominence in defence and strategic planning but extends its influence profoundly into the realms of business and technology as well.

The term "unknown unknown" was popularized by former United States Secretary of Defence Mr. Donald Rumsfeld during a Department of Defence news briefing in 2002. He used it in the context of discussing the lack of evidence linking the government of Iraq with the supply of weapons of mass destruction to terrorist groups.

Rumsfeld stated:

"There are known knowns; there are things we know we know. We also know there are known unknowns; that is to say we know there are some things we do not know. But there are also *unknown unknowns*—the ones we don't know we don't know."

The *unknown knowns* & *unknown unknowns* are the factors or problems that exist beyond the horizon of our current knowledge and expectation, rendering them particularly challenging to plan for or predict.

To cite, I can say that the emergence of COVID-19 pandemic serves as a stark reminder of the disruptive potential of *unknown unknowns*, which drastically altered market dynamics and caught many businesses off guard.

While these enigmatic elements pose significant threats, they also present unparalleled opportunities for innovation and competitive advantage. For an example, the Blockchain technology, *once an unknown unknown,* emerged from obscurity to revolutionize multiple industries, from finance to supply chain management.

A Framework for Understanding - 2x2 Matrix of Awareness Vs Knowledge:

To provide more clarity and understanding, I created the 2x2 matrix of knowns and unknowns, distinguishing between known knowns, known unknowns, unknown knowns, and unknown unknowns.

This matrix is the foundation of our exploration and serves as a guide for businesses to categorize and approach the spectrum of challenges and opportunities they face.

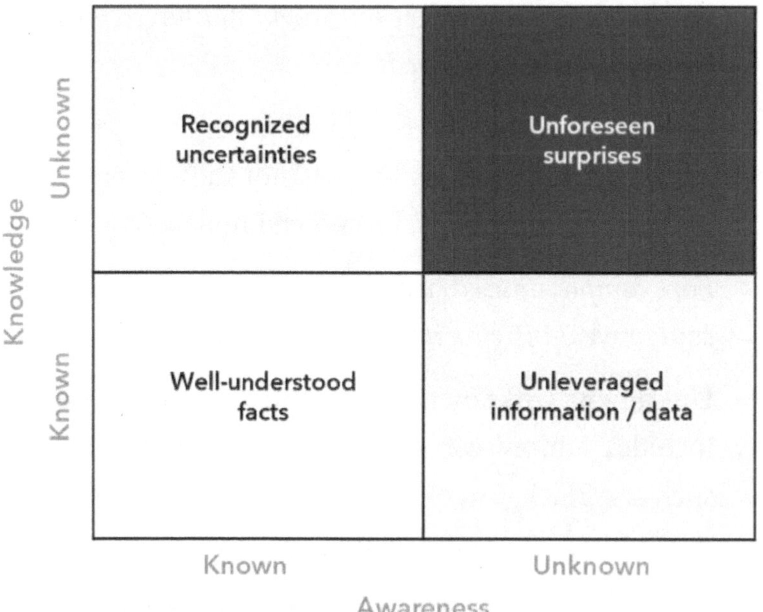

Fig 5.1: Matrix of awareness & Knowledge

Let us explore each of these four scenarios, with examples.

- **Known Knowns:** These are the aspects of business and market dynamics that are well-understood and predictable.

  For instance, consumer behavior patterns during major holidays are typically well-documented and anticipated by retailers.

- **Known Unknowns:** Challenges or questions that are recognized but lack definitive answers fall into this category.

  A tech start-up may be aware of potential regulatory hurdles in a new market but might not have clarity on how they will be enforced.

- **Unknown Knowns:** Information or data that an organization possesses but has not fully leveraged or understood represents, unknown knowns.

  For example, unused customer feedback that, if analyzed, could reveal insights into product improvements.

- **Unknown Unknowns:** The most elusive category includes unforeseen challenges and opportunities, such as Black Swan events, that are impossible to predict and often have significant impacts.

  The COVID-19 pandemic is a prime example, drastically altering global business landscapes with little warning.

Next, we will see how to successfully overcome the challenges we may face while exploring the unknown knowns and unknown unknowns.

Strategies to Overcome the Challenges

1. To navigate the murky waters of unknown knowns & unknown unknowns, businesses must employ proactive research and analysis techniques as well as curiosity-led thinking.
2. Constant scanning of the external & internal environment for signals of change—emerging technologies, societal shifts, regulatory changes—is essential.
3. Techniques such as scenario planning, horizon scanning, start with the 'why' and challenge the 'status quo', can help you to anticipate the future developments and prepare you for various outcomes.

Food for thought:

- Failure reasons list:

  As a matter of fact, how many organizations and leaderships are willing to list down the complete laundry list of why their business plan will fail? The entire syllabus for resilience can be culled out if this exercise is resorted to by corporate leaderships during every year's budget / business planning sessions. Such a list will serve as a monitoring blueprint which can be discussed during the monthly review meetings.

- Hidden talents of In-house experts:

  How many organizations have the culture and habit of analysing the external environment and harness the knowledge of in-house subject matter experts irrespective of the role they play in the organization? Such initiatives will not only serve to enrich their jobs but also recognize various hidden talents in the organization. Having a practice of sharing knowledge once a month will uplift the collective talent within the organization and strongly push forward the resilience agenda for the organization.

In addition to thinking and implementing the above processes, it will be my suggestion to practice <u>curiosity-led data analytics</u> as well. This can play a pivotal role in identifying 'unknown knowns' by uncovering patterns and trends that elude human perception. Simple analysis to AI led analytics can also come handy. It is proven that Machine learning algorithms can process vast amounts of data to predict potential disruptions or identify emerging consumer needs. For example, AI-driven social listening tools can reveal shifts in consumer sentiment that signal emerging market trends.

A leader will demonstrate exceptional quality if these

suggestions are taken into their problem finding pursuits.

Let us learn more about using a tested and proven framework for exploring the unknown knowns and unknown unknowns, in the next section.

Navigating the Unknown Knowns

To make it clearer, I will say "Unknown Knowns" refer to information that exists within an entity but has not been effectively recognized or utilized. *Identifying and leveraging these dormant assets can catalyse innovation, enhance strategic decision-making, and sharpen competitive edges.*

In my experience as a business consultant, I have seen, organizations often sitting on a wealth of underutilized data and knowledge, obscured by operational silos and a reluctance to challenge the status quo.

It may be that siloed departments, guarding their data without understanding its broader applicability, coupled with a lack of curiosity and an aversion to data analytics, hinder the exploration of valuable insights.

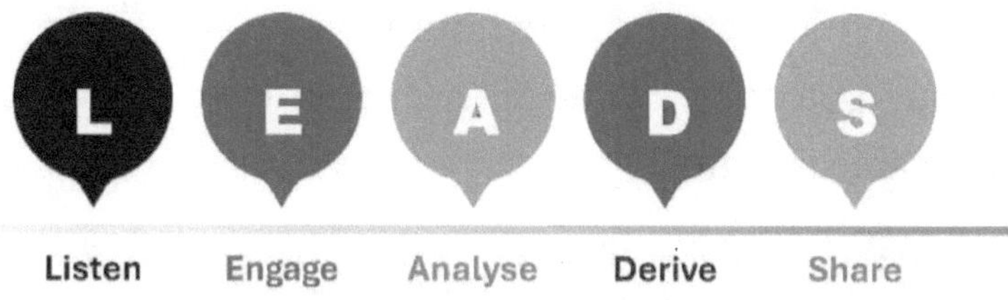

Fig 5.2: Design thinking approach adapted for problem finding

The above visually depicted process is a simple design thinking approach that can be emulated to problem finding. (*Several real-life cases studies are shared in chapter 13 to derive greater understanding on the unknown knowns and the way to deal with them*).

Here, I will explain this framework step by step making it easier to follow:

Step 1: Listen

Adopting an open-minded diagnostic approach is critical in revealing these hidden issues. To achieve that a multifaceted examination of the organization, starting with a comprehensive listening exercise is needed where stakeholders share their *perspectives on various business aspects, symptoms, and issues.*

Step 2: Engage

Next, initiating an engagement with key stakeholders to assess data capabilities sets the stage for in-depth analysis. Identifying relevant data sources to accurately depict the business landscape becomes imperative at this juncture. Searching for siloed data within the organization reveals hidden potential; connecting disparate data can yield invaluable insights.

This step is pivotal – uncovering data that are unconnected but directly or indirectly impact overall results. Subject matter expertise proves critical, coupled with a sense of curiosity for experimentation.

These skills become indispensable when collaborating with diverse stakeholders to identify data and discern their interconnected patterns.

Step 3: Analyse

The next step is assimilating this data to create a multidimensional model that best represents the business, laying the groundwork for *insightful data preparation.*

Step 4: Derive

A critical examination of the data can reveal symptoms and indications of deeper problems. By deriving accurate insights and inferences, the real issues that may have been veiled by surface-level symptoms become clearer.

Step 5: Share

The final step involves sharing these insights in a way that promotes easy comprehension and facilitates immediate action. Effective storytelling is a powerful tool that helps stakeholders understand the implications of the insights, enabling them to make informed decisions swiftly.

Let's find out how to deal with the Unknown unknowns.

Navigating Unknown Unknowns

The unpredictability of Black Swan events, such as the COVID-19 pandemic, underscores the necessity for businesses to develop strategies that account for unknown unknowns.

For instance, companies that had diversified their supply chains prior to the pandemic were able to mitigate some of the disruptions caused by global lockdowns, exemplifying the value of preparedness in an uncertain world.

Similarly, sensing the brewing tensions between Ukraine and Russia, some companies diversified their sourcing from that region. They were able to de-risk supply shortages and ensure smooth production cycles.

(Read the dedicated chapter 9 – Preparing for the Unknown Unknowns for more discussion on this).

There are two steps I can suggest here in strategizing for unknown unknowns.

1. Preparing for the Unpredictable

The cornerstone of navigating unknown unknowns lies in building resilient and adaptive systems. This entails creating flexible strategies capable of pivoting in response to unexpected changes and fostering a culture of agility and continuous learning within the organization.

Implementing modular systems and processes that can be quickly reconfigured enhances a company's ability to respond to unforeseen challenges.

2. Anticipating the Unpredictable

Continuous adaptation is a key corporate imperative. The analogy of 'seeing a U-turn from a distance while driving' highlights the importance of preparation. By employing problem-finding techniques and keeping a vigilant eye on external developments through frameworks like PESTEL*, businesses can position themselves to navigate the sudden changes with greater agility.

This proactive stance, characterized by "adaptation on the go," is increasingly vital for corporate leaders in today's fast-paced world.

We can see here two of the most popular case studies.

Shining a Light on Success Stories

1. Netflix's Pivot to Streaming: Originally a DVD rental service, Netflix foresaw the potential of streaming technology—an unknown unknown at the time—to revolutionize the entertainment industry. By pivoting to streaming early on, Netflix outpaced competitors and fundamentally altered how content is consumed.

---

*(*Political Economical Social Technological Environmental & Legal analysis)*

2. SpaceX's Reusable Rockets: SpaceX ventured into the unknown by developing reusable rocket technology, defying the industry norm of one-time-use boosters. This innovation significantly reduced the cost of space travel, opening new possibilities for exploration and commerce beyond Earth's atmosphere.

Conclusion: A possibility into the future

The exploration of unknown knowns and unknown unknowns is a journey into the uncharted territories of business and technology. While these challenges may seem daunting, they also hold the promise of unparalleled innovation and growth. By embracing the unknown and harnessing its transformative potential, businesses can steer with confidence and resilience.

Through vigilance, agility, and a forward-looking mindset, organizations can not only navigate the fog of uncertainty but also emerge as pioneers, shaping the future of their industries.

06

Cultivating a Problem Finding Mindset

In the corporate world, success hinges on the ability to identify and address problems before they become roadblocks. But simply recognizing issues isn't enough. It is essential to cultivate a problem-finding mindset for uncovering hidden challenges, sparking innovation, and driving continuous improvement.

This chapter delves into the psychological aspects of problem finding - understanding the mental barriers - equips you with various techniques to cultivate a valuable skillset, and showcases real-world examples of companies that are reaping the rewards of practicing exceptional problem-finding culture in their organizations. Let us see each one of them in detail.

A. Understanding the hindrances

Our brains are wired for efficiency, relying on cognitive biases – mental shortcuts – to make quick decisions.

Three such cognitive biases include 1) confirmation bias 2) anchoring bias 3) status quo bias.

However, these biases can sometimes hinder our ability to identify problems effectively.

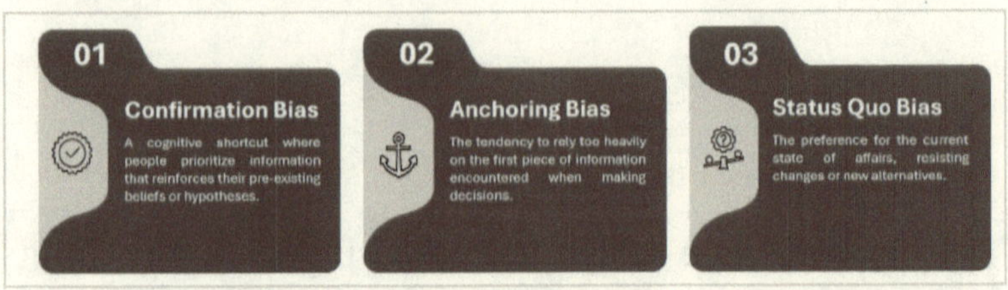

Fig: 6.1: Three Cognitive biases

1. Confirmation Bias

It is a natural human tendency to favour information that confirms our existing beliefs which is called Confirmation Bias.

To overcome this bias, you must challenge yourself by actively seeking out dissenting viewpoints. Should encourage team discussions and brainstorming sessions with diverse perspectives among employees.

E.g. Imagine a sales team consistently exceeding targets. Their manager, influenced by confirmation bias, might believe their strategy is perfect. However, an open-minded approach could involve surveying customers to understand unmet needs. This could reveal opportunities for product improvement or service expansion, leading to even greater success.

2. Anchoring Bias

Anchoring bias is indeed another natural human tendency where individuals give disproportionate weight to the first piece of information they receive about a topic.

This initial piece of information, or "anchor," influences subsequent judgments and decisions more than it should, even if more relevant or accurate information is presented later. Leadership qualities are tested here to take a bold decision sometimes to overcome this bias.

E.g. A software company is launching a new product and in the first sales meeting, the sales manager suggests a price point of $99 per user per month based on initial cost estimates. As the team further discusses pricing strategies and competitor analysis, they find evidence suggesting that the market could bear a price of up to $150 per user. However, due to the initial suggestion of $99, the team struggles to consider the higher price point seriously. They are anchored to the $99 figure, and even though it's rational to set a higher price based on the added features and market readiness, they decide on a launch price of $110, potentially leaving significant revenue on the table. This example shows how an early figure can disproportionately influence final pricing decisions, even in the face of contradictory evidence.

3. Status Quo Bias

This bias can be explained where one prefers to maintain the current state as it gives comfort to be in that state rather than stepping into unknown areas.

To overcome this, one should not be afraid to question the existing practices and processes. Implementing mechanisms for gathering employee feedback on potential pain points will help to change the status quo bias among the employees.

E.g. A traditional publishing company has been relying on the same business model for decades: selling books through brick-and-mortar stores and a basic online ordering system. Despite the publishing industry's clear shift towards digital platforms and e-books, the company's leadership is hesitant to invest in a full digital transformation. They prefer to stick with the familiar business model, fearing the risks of change, even as they lose market share to more digitally savvy competitors.

B. Cultivating the Mindset:

Moving beyond biases requires cultivating intellectual curiosity. Here are some ways to do that:

- Embrace a Growth Mindset: Believe that intelligence and capabilities can be developed through dedication and effort. Promote learning opportunities within the organization.

- Practice Purposeful Listening: Pay close attention to what others are saying without interrupting.
- Ask Open-Ended Questions: Prompt deeper thinking and encourage employees to share unique perspectives.

C. Developing the Skill Set

A problem-finding mindset is complemented by a strong skillset. Honing these areas will help:

- Critical Thinking: Analyze information objectively by breaking down problems into smaller components. Consider cause-and-effect relationships and potential consequences of various solutions.
- Creative Exploration: Don't settle for the first solution that comes to mind. Employ brainstorming techniques like mind-mapping to generate a wide range of possibilities. This visual representation helps generate ideas and identify potential connections between them.

D. Techniques for Enhancing Observational Skills:

- Active Observation: Go beyond simply looking; pay close attention to details, processes, & interactions.
    - *Example: In a retail store, observe customer behavior. Do they struggle to find products? Do they seem confused about store layout?*

- Asking "Why?": Challenge assumptions and probe deeper to understand the root causes of inefficiencies.
    - *Example: If a customer service line has long wait times, ask "Why?" Is it understaffing, inefficient call routing, or a lack of self-service options?*
- Seeking Diverse Input: Gather insights from colleagues across different departments to gain a more holistic view of the organization.
    - *Example: Talk to sales, marketing, and customer service teams to understand their unique perspectives on customer satisfaction.*
- Utilizing Data Visualization Tools: Data can reveal hidden patterns and trends that might not be readily apparent. Tools like charts, graphs, and dashboards can help identify areas for improvement.
    - *Example: Analyze website traffic data to see which pages have high bounce rates. This could indicate usability issues or a lack of relevant content.*

E. Innovative Thinking:

There are many examples out there to show how innovative thinking will help in developing problem finding mindset and in turn how it helps businesses to succeed. Listing out some illustrations to demonstrate the effect of innovative thinking.

Illustration 1: Airbnb - Rethinking Hospitality: Founded in 2008, Airbnb disrupted the hospitality industry by leveraging underutilized resources – people's spare rooms.

The founders identified a problem: On one side expensive, limited hotel options for travelers and on the other side, a lack of income opportunity for property owners with unused space. They solved it by rethinking hospitality.

- **Initial Challenges:** Airbnb faced initial resistance from the hospitality industry and concerns about safety and security.
- **Problem-Solving Approach:** Airbnb built a robust platform for trust and security, including user verification, reviews, and insurance policies. They focused on creating a unique travel experience that allowed for cultural immersion and connection with local communities.
- **Key Takeaways:**
    - Challenge industry norms and identify opportunities to utilize existing resources more effectively.
    - Embrace technology to create a solution that caters to a broader range of customer needs.

Illustration 2: Netflix - Revolutionizing Entertainment

Netflix recognized the limitations of traditional video rental stores – late fees, limited selection, and inconvenient return policies.

They saw an opportunity to leverage the growing internet bandwidth and consumer desire for convenience.

- **Initial Challenges:** Netflix had to compete with established brick-and-mortar video rental stores and convince customers to adopt a new streaming model.
- **Problem-Solving Approach:** Netflix offered a subscription-based service with a vast library of movies and TV shows available for instant streaming. They personalized user experiences with recommendations based on viewing history and invested heavily in original content creation to stand out from competitors.
- **Key Takeaways:**
    - Be at the forefront of technological change and anticipate customer needs before they arise.
    - Focus on creating a seamless and personalized user experience.

Illustration 3: Tesla - Electrifying Transportation

Tesla identified the limitations of traditional gasoline-powered vehicles – environmental pollution and dependence on fossil fuels.

They envisioned a future of sustainable transportation powered by electric vehicles.

- **Initial Challenges:** Tesla faced scepticism about the practicality and range of electric vehicles, as well as the need for a robust charging infrastructure.
- **Problem-Solving Approach:** Tesla focused on innovation, developing high-performance electric vehicles with extended ranges. They built a network of Supercharger stations for long-distance travel and partnered with businesses and municipalities to expand charging accessibility.
- **Key Takeaways:**
  - Think disruptively and address challenges with bold solutions.
  - Invest in research and development to create innovative products that cater to a sustainable future.

Illustration 4: Khan Academy - Democratizing Education

Khan Academy emerged in response to a critical challenge in traditional education: the lack of personalized learning. Traditional classrooms often employ a one-size-fits-all approach, leaving students who learn at different paces feeling frustrated or bored.

Initial Challenges: Khan Academy faced the challenge of disrupting established education systems and convincing educators and parents of the value of online learning.

Problem-Solving Approach: Khan Academy addressed this problem by creating a free, online platform offering a vast library of educational resources. These resources include short, engaging video lessons, interactive practice exercises, and personalized learning tools.

Key Takeaways:

- Removed the barriers of cost and location, making high-quality education accessible to anyone with an internet connection.
- Use of technology to create adaptive learning environments.

These examples clearly show that by developing a problem-finding mindset, companies can turn challenges into opportunities for innovation and growth.

Conclusion: Developing the mindset to identify opportunities

The journey of problem finding is one of continual exploration, adaptation, and innovation. By understanding the hindrances, developing essential skill sets, and employing techniques for enhancing observational skills, organizations can unlock hidden opportunities and drive continuous improvement.

Through real-world illustrations, we have witnessed the transformative power of problem finding, from disrupting industries to democratizing education.

It is very important to foster a culture of curiosity, critical thinking, and collaboration to empower the businesses in these challenging times to move from problem solving to problem finding mindset.

07

Fostering a Culture of Curiosity

Curiosity is ingrained in human nature from the earliest stages of development. During infancy, children are consumed by an insatiable curiosity, eagerly exploring their surroundings and eagerly absorbing new experiences. However, as individuals progress through life, societal norms and expectations can stifle this innate curiosity, relegating it to the background. Yet, curiosity remains fundamental to human existence, serving as the catalyst for key future skills such as creativity, adaptability, and flexibility.

By recognizing the importance of curiosity and cultivating it within their organizations, businesses can empower individuals to thrive in the future of work driving innovation and creativity, and to tackle challenges with confidence and resilience driving positive changes. The effects are discussed in detail here.

A. The Importance of Curiosity in the Future of Work

Recent research and insights from the World Economic Forum underscore the critical role of curiosity in shaping the future of work. As technology continues to advance and industries undergo rapid transformations, individuals who possess a curious mindset are better equipped to adapt to change, learn new skills, and navigate uncertainty. Curiosity fuels lifelong learning and enables individuals to stay ahead in a dynamic and ever-evolving job market.

The visual schematic below encapsulates the six future-forward fundamentals that underscore the importance of curiosity in shaping the future of work.

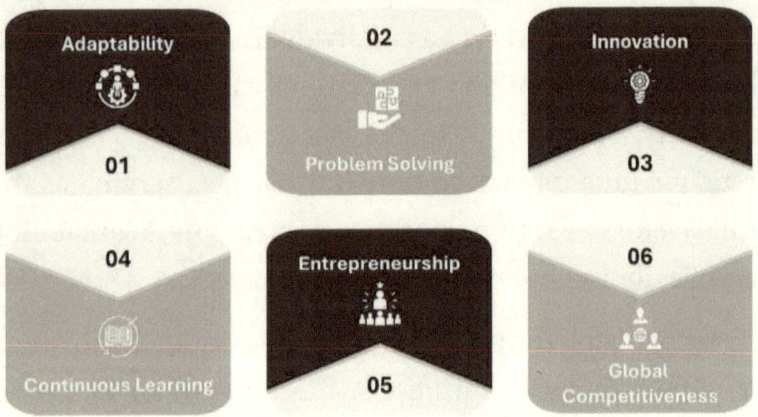

Fig: 7.1: 6 Future Forward Fundamentals: Importance of Curiosity in shaping the future of work

- **Adaptability:** Curiosity enables individuals to adapt to new technologies, industries, and job roles. In a world where job requirements are constantly evolving, individuals who possess a curious mindset are better equipped to learn new skills and navigate transitions with ease. (*Refer Page: 68 for more details on Curiosity and adaptability*)

- **Problem-Solving:** Curiosity drives effective problem-solving by encouraging individuals to ask questions, explore alternatives, and seek innovative solutions. Curious individuals are more likely to approach challenges with an open mind and a willingness to experiment, leading to more robust problem-solving outcomes.

- **Innovation:** Curiosity fuels innovation by inspiring individuals to explore new ideas, challenge assumptions, and connect disparate concepts. In today's competitive market, organizations that foster a culture of curiosity are better positioned to drive innovation and stay ahead of the curve.

- **Continuous Learning:** Curious individuals are lifelong learners, constantly seeking out new knowledge and experiences. In a rapidly changing job market, the ability to adapt and learn continuously is essential for staying relevant and advancing in one's career.

- **Entrepreneurship:** Curiosity is a hallmark of successful entrepreneurs, driving them to identify opportunities, take risks, and pursue their passions. By fostering curiosity among employees, organizations can unlock entrepreneurial potential and drive innovation from within.

- **Global Competitiveness:** In an increasingly interconnected world, curiosity is essential for understanding diverse cultures, markets, and perspectives. Individuals who possess a curious mindset are better equipped to navigate global challenges and seize opportunities in the international marketplace.

B. Curiosity as a Driver of Innovation and Creativity

Innovation and creativity are the lifeblood of successful organizations, driving growth, competitiveness, and sustainability. Curiosity plays a crucial role in fueling innovation and creativity by inspiring individuals to explore new ideas, challenge assumptions, and think outside the box.

The visual representation below elucidates the curiosity catalysts that are driving innovation and creativity.

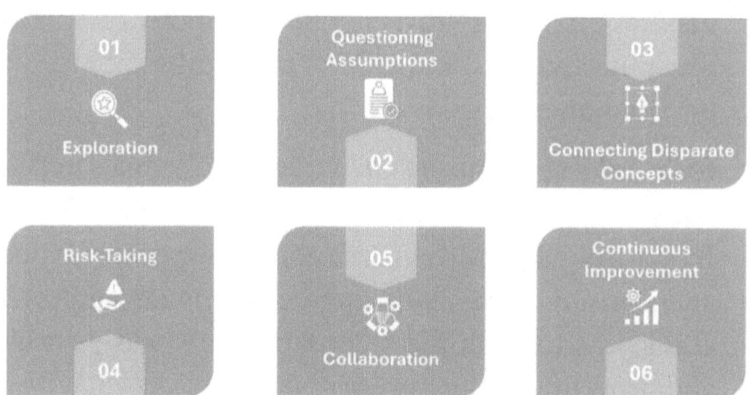

Fig 7.2: Curiosity catalyst for driving innovation & creativity

- **Exploration:** Curious individuals are natural explorers, constantly seeking out new experiences, ideas, and perspectives. By encouraging exploration and experimentation, organizations can tap into the creative potential of their teams and uncover new opportunities for innovation.
- **Questioning Assumptions:** Curiosity prompts individuals to question assumptions and challenge the status quo. By challenging conventional wisdom and exploring alternative viewpoints, curious individuals can uncover hidden insights and drive innovative solutions to complex problems.
- **Connecting Disparate Concepts:** Curiosity fosters connections between seemingly unrelated concepts, leading to breakthrough innovations. By drawing

inspiration from diverse fields, industries, and disciplines, curious individuals can synthesize ideas in new and unexpected ways.

- **Risk-Taking:** Curiosity encourages individuals to take risks and embrace uncertainty in pursuit of new ideas. By creating a culture that celebrates experimentation and learning from failure, organizations can empower employees to push the boundaries of what's possible and drive innovation forward.
- **Collaboration:** Curiosity fosters collaboration by bringing together individuals with diverse backgrounds, perspectives, and expertise. By creating opportunities for cross-disciplinary collaboration and knowledge sharing, organizations can harness the collective creativity of their teams and drive innovation at scale.
- **Continuous Improvement:** Curiosity drives continuous improvement in problem-solving by encouraging individuals to reflect on past experiences, learn from mistakes, and iterate on their approaches. Curious problem-solvers are constantly refining their methods, incorporating feedback, and striving for excellence in their quest to solve complex challenges.

C. Curiosity and Adaptability

Curiosity plays a central role in enabling individuals to adapt well to navigate uncertainty, embrace change, and thrive, in diverse environments.

The visual depiction below illustrates the adaptive advantages nurtured through curiosity.

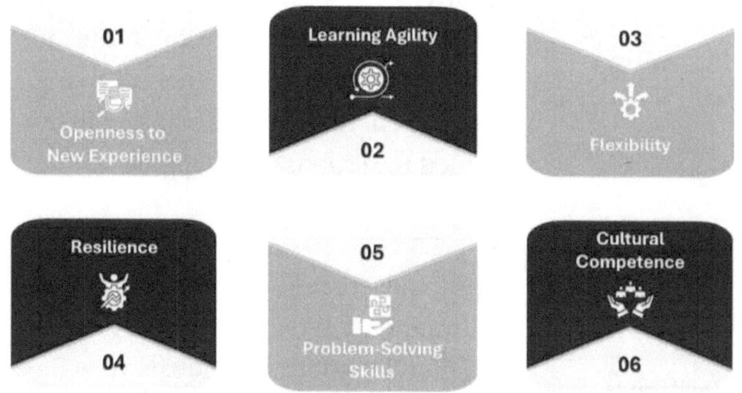

Fig 7.3: Adaptive advantages of curiosity

Openness to New Experiences	Curious individuals are open to new experiences and eager to explore unfamiliar territories. This openness enables them to adapt quickly to new situations, environments, and challenges, without being hindered by fear or resistance.
Learning Agility	Curiosity fosters learning agility by encouraging individuals to seek out new knowledge, skills, and perspectives. Curious learners are constantly expanding their horizons, experimenting with different approaches, and adapting their strategies based on feedback and experience.

Flexibility:	Curiosity promotes flexibility by encouraging individuals to consider alternative viewpoints, adapt their strategies, and embrace diverse perspectives. Curious individuals are less rigid in their thinking, allowing them to pivot and adjust course as needed in response to changing circumstances.
Resilience	Curiosity fosters resilience by instilling a growth mindset and a willingness to learn from failure. Curious individuals view setbacks as opportunities for growth and development, enabling them to bounce back quickly and adapt in the face of adversity.
Problem-Solving Skills	Curiosity enhances problem-solving skills by encouraging individuals to approach challenges with a curious mindset, asking questions, exploring alternatives, and experimenting with different solutions. This problem-solving agility enables individuals to adapt to changing circumstances and overcome obstacles with ease.

Cultural Competence	Curiosity encourages individuals to seek out diverse perspectives, understand different cultures, and adapt their behaviours and communication styles, accordingly. Curious individuals are better equipped to navigate cross-cultural interactions, build rapport with diverse stakeholders, and thrive in multicultural environments.

D. Overcoming Barriers to Curiosity

While curiosity is a valuable skill, it can be hindered by various barriers, including fear of failure, complacency, and lack of support. Organizations must actively work to overcome these barriers and create an environment where curiosity is valued, supported, and rewarded to unleash the full potential of their teams and drive innovation, creativity, and success in the workplace.

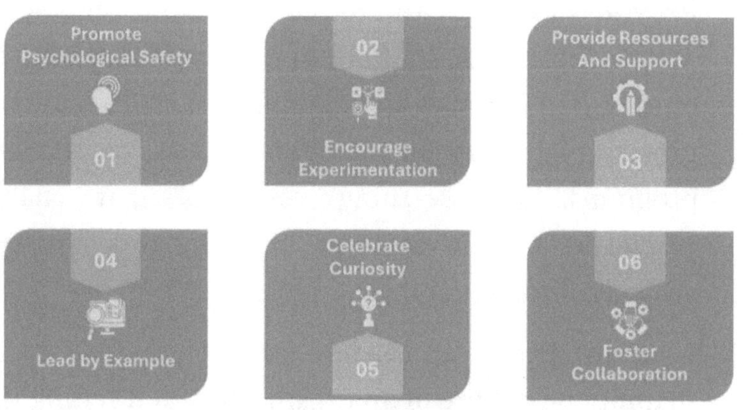

Fig 7.4: Measures for overcoming barriers to curiosity

The visual above shows the six barrier-breaking measures that are crucial for overcoming obstacles to curiosity and for fostering a culture of exploration. Let's discuss them here.

1. **Promote Psychological Safety:** Create a culture of psychological safety where individuals feel comfortable taking risks, asking questions, and challenging the status quo without fear of judgment or reprisal. When employees feel safe to express their curiosity and experiment with new ideas, they are more likely to unleash their full potential and drive innovation.

2. **Encourage Experimentation:** Provide opportunities for employees to experiment, explore, and learn from failure. Encourage a mindset of experimentation and iteration, where employees are empowered to try new approaches, gather feedback, and refine their ideas based on what they learn along the way.

3. **Provide Resources and Support:** Provide employees with the resources, training, and support they need to pursue their interests and develop new skills. Invest in professional development opportunities, mentorship programs, and learning resources that enable employees to cultivate their curiosity and continue growing throughout their careers.

4. **Lead by Example:** Leaders play a crucial role in shaping the culture of an organization and setting the tone for curiosity. Lead by example by demonstrating

a curious mindset, asking questions, seeking out new experiences, and encouraging others to do the same. When leaders prioritize curiosity and lifelong learning, it sends a powerful message to employees about its importance and value within the organization.

5. **Celebrate Curiosity:** Recognize and celebrate individuals who demonstrate curiosity and initiative in their work. Highlight success stories of curiosity-driven innovation and reward employees who take risks, ask questions, and explore new ideas. By celebrating curiosity, organizations reinforce its value and create an environment where it is encouraged and rewarded.

6. **Foster Collaboration:** Encourage collaboration and knowledge sharing among employees by creating opportunities for cross-functional teams to work together on projects and initiatives. Foster a culture of collaboration where individuals are encouraged to seek out diverse perspectives, share their ideas, and collaborate with others to achieve common goals. By fostering collaboration, organizations can harness the collective intelligence of their teams and drive innovation forward.

Conclusion: Curiosity – The bedrock of innovation

Curiosity is not only a trait to be cultivated in the workplace, but also a fundamental aspect of human development and lifelong learning. While curiosity is innate in children, fueling exploration and learning, societal norms and education often dampen it over time. This is unfortunate, as curiosity is a critical skill in today's complex world. And rapid technological advancements necessitate continuous learning, and fostering curiosity is key to unlocking this potential.

Incorporating curiosity into problem finding and solution-building processes can lead to transformative outcomes. By asking unconventional questions, considering diverse viewpoints, and encouraging experimentation, we discover innovative solutions. Curiosity fosters collaboration, openness, and continuous improvement - all essential for driving innovation.

As organizations strive to adapt to the demands of the future of work, fostering a culture of curiosity becomes paramount. Leaders play a crucial role in cultivating a culture of curiosity. By encouraging their teams to question, challenge assumptions, and embrace new ideas, they empower individuals to unlock their potential and drive meaningful change.

Ultimately, curiosity isn't just a trait - it's a learnable skill that drives innovation, creativity, and adaptability. By embracing curiosity in problem finding, organizations can unlock new possibilities, inspire breakthrough solutions, and ultimately, thrive in an ever-changing world.

08

Anticipating the Future - Problem Finding in Strategic Planning

With rapid technological advancements, geopolitical shifts, and global challenges reshaping the industry environments at an exceptional pace, we are witnessing unprecedented levels of unpredictability. Added to that the interconnectedness of our world means that every action, every decision, has far-reaching implications, often in ways that are difficult to foresee.

This is the kind of future we are facing – one characterized by uncertainty, complexity, and rapid change. In this dynamic environment, the ability to anticipate the future and integrate it into strategic planning processes is more critical than ever. Organizations must not only adapt to change but also anticipate it, proactively identifying emerging trends, risks, and opportunities to stay ahead of the curve.

But how do we anticipate the future in a world where the only certainty is uncertainty? How do we navigate the interconnected web of factors shaping our world, from technological innovation to socio-economic trends to environmental challenges? And most importantly, how do we translate this understanding of the future into actionable strategies that drive success and resilience?

In this chapter I explored how problem finding can be integrated into strategic planning processes to anticipate the future, align with business objectives, and build agile and resilient organizations.

We will examine tools and methodologies for anticipating future trends and challenges, such as scenario planning and trend analysis, and explore how organizations can integrate problem finding into their strategic planning processes to build agility and resilience in the face of uncertainty.

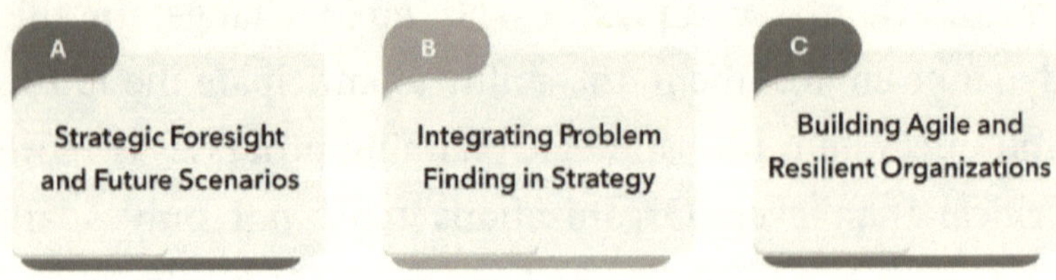

Fig: 8.1: Tools and methodologies for anticipating future trends

In the face of rapid change and unpredictability, the ability to foresee the future and adapt strategically is no longer a luxury but a necessity. Embracing problem finding as a core component of strategic planning is the way forward for the organizations to face the complexities of the future with confidence and positioning themselves for success.

Let's explore the ways to include problem finding in the strategic planning.

A. Strategic Foresight and Future Scenarios

Strategic foresight involves systematically exploring the future to identify emerging trends, risks, and opportunities that may impact an organization's strategic direction.

Future scenarios help organizations anticipate various possible futures and develop strategies to navigate them effectively.

In the post-COVID era, the global order is continuously and rapidly evolving, opening both opportunities and risks. Opportunities present themselves when we keep a close eye on developments, allowing us to act swiftly and adaptively. Conversely, risks surface if we overlook early indications, potentially giving rise to challenges down the line. As corporate leaders, it is crucial to continuously analyze these ongoing changes and adapt on-the-go.

Tools for Anticipating Future Trends and Challenges:

- Environmental scanning: There should be a regular monitoring of external factors such as market trends, technological advancements, and regulatory changes to identify emerging opportunities and threats.

(This aspect has assumed critical importance post-COVID. Next chapter - Preparing for the Unknown Unknowns- extensively delves into specific topics of today's relevance, which typically do not find a place in boardroom discussions or strategic business planning sessions).

- Trend analysis: Analyzing historical data and patterns to forecast future trends and anticipate shifts in consumer behavior, market dynamics, and industry trends.
- Delphi method: Engaging experts in iterative rounds of surveys and feedback to generate insights and consensus on future scenarios and trends.

B. Integrating Problem Finding in Strategy

Integrating problem finding into strategic planning processes ensures that organizations focus on identifying and addressing critical challenges and opportunities that align with their long-term objectives and vision.

By doing so, stakeholders can anticipate evolving opportunities and threats, thereby preparing the organization to a reasonable extent for potential incidents that may occur.

This approach ensures that the organization is better prepared, *akin to becoming aware of a U-turn 500 meters ahead of the actual curve, while driving.*

Aligning Problem Finding with Business Objectives:

It is also important to associate the problem finding focus of the organization is in tandem with their different objectives. Let's consider,

- Vision and mission alignment: Ensuring that problem finding activities are aligned with the organization's vision, mission, and strategic goals will help to drive meaningful impact and value creation.
- Strategic priorities: Identifying key strategic priorities and focus areas that require problem finding efforts will help to address critical business challenges, capitalize on emerging opportunities, and to drive innovation.

C. Building Agile and Resilient Organizations

Agility and resilience are essential for organizations to thrive amidst today's constant change and disruption. Problem finding plays a crucial role in building adaptive and resilient organizations capable of responding effectively.

Keeping pace with constant and rapid changes can only occur when organizations possess the ability to adapt on-the-go. However, this is not an easy feat. It's equivalent to asking a car mechanic to tune the engine while the car is in motion.

Adaptability in the Face of Change:

Every organization can build adaptability by inculcating certain behavioural practices.

- Organizational culture: Fostering a culture of continuous learning, experimentation, and adaptation to encourage employees to embrace change and innovation.
- Agile methodologies: Adopting agile practices to enable teams to respond quickly to changing market conditions and customer needs.

We can prepare for uncertainty and complexity by implementing robust risk management processes and strategies to identify, assess, and mitigate potential risks and uncertainties that may impact organizational performance and resilience. Also, by developing contingency plans and alternative courses of action to navigate them effectively.

Conclusion: Strategizing for future challenges

By integrating problem finding into strategic planning processes, organizations can anticipate future challenges and opportunities, align with business objectives, and build agile and resilient organizations capable of thriving amidst uncertainty and change.

09

Preparing for the Unknown Unknowns

Our experiences tell that an ever-changing array of external forces shapes the modern enterprises and the issues they face. These external forces can range from changes in geopolitics to innovations in technology. There are disruptions to operations, changes to market dynamics and highly competitive environment are all possible outcomes of these pressures.

In this complicated environment, being strategically prepared is crucial for organisations that want to succeed when encountered with unpredictability.

In this chapter, I would like to discuss in depth about the five global factors that drive the uncertainty and complexity in the present RUPT[@] world and how businesses can prepare themselves to face the challenges in a better manner.

As we all are aware, PESTEL analysis, an acronym for Political, Economic, Social, Technological, Environmental, and Legal factors, provides a comprehensive framework

---

(@introduced by Creative Leadership Institute, UK)

for assessing the external environment and identifying potential opportunities and threats. By systematically analyzing each of these factors, organizations can gain valuable insights into the forces shaping their operating environment and develop strategies to adapt and thrive in the face of change. Let us understand its crucial role in strategic adaptation, in this section.

A. The Crucial Role of PESTEL Analysis in Strategic Adaptation

At its core, PESTEL analysis serves as a compass, guiding organizational strategy and decision-making by providing a holistic view of the external landscape. *Unlike traditional strategic planning exercises, which often focus solely on internal capabilities and market dynamics, PESTEL analysis broadens the scope to include factors that may lie beyond the organization's immediate control but can nonetheless have a significant impact on its success.*

One of the key benefits of PESTEL analysis is its ability to facilitate strategic adaptation on-the-go. Rather than treating it as a one-time exercise or a mere academic exercise to fill presentation slides, organizations should view PESTEL analysis as a living document—a dynamic tool that evolves with changes in the external environment. Rather than being relegated to a shelf or forgotten after the completion of a strategic planning session, PESTEL analysis should be regularly revisited, updated, and integrated into ongoing strategic discussions and decision-making processes.

A best practice in this regard is to designate a dedicated individual or department responsible for overseeing the ongoing monitoring and analysis of external factors. This individual or team, often housed within the excellence department or strategy function, serves as the custodian of the PESTEL analysis, continuously monitoring changes in the external environment, identifying emerging trends and risks, and mapping them to the organization's strategy and operations.

By embedding PESTEL analysis into the fabric of the organization and institutionalizing a culture of strategic adaptation, organizations can better anticipate changes in the external environment, proactively identify strategic opportunities, and mitigate potential risks. Moreover, by aligning strategy with the evolving external landscape, organizations can enhance their resilience, agility, and long-term sustainability in an increasingly volatile and uncertain world.

B. Navigating Global Uncertainties: Key Forces and Strategic Preparedness

As globalization continues to accelerate, businesses find themselves operating in an environment characterized by unprecedented interconnectedness. While globalization has unlocked new growth opportunities and expanded market access, it has also exposed organizations to a host of risks stemming from geopolitical tensions, economic fluctuations, and regulatory changes.

The COVID-19 pandemic served as a stark reminder of the fragility of global supply chains and the importance of resilience in the face of unforeseen disruptions. Indeed, the pandemic was a classic example of an "unknown unknown"—a black swan event that caught many businesses off guard and underscored the need for robust contingency planning and strategic foresight.

From the rise of protectionist policies to the emergence of disruptive technologies, organizations are constantly confronted with new threats and opportunities that demand careful consideration and strategic response.

At the heart of this response lies the concept of strategic preparedness—a proactive approach to identifying, assessing, and mitigating risks, while also capitalizing on emerging trends and opportunities.

The five key global factors—de-dollarization, deglobalization, Artificial Intelligence (AI), rise in global conflicts, and population dynamics—stand out as particularly salient drivers of uncertainty and disruption.

Each of these factors has the potential to exert a profound

impact on businesses across industries, reshaping market dynamics, influencing consumer behavior, and altering competitive dynamics.

By understanding these forces and taking proactive steps to anticipate and respond to the change, organizations can position themselves to thrive amidst uncertainty and emerge stronger in the face of adversity.

Let's delve deeper into each of these key global factors, exploring their significance and potential implications for businesses and learn some actionable strategies for preparedness.

Note: *There can be several other factors assuming equal importance as these five or more or less. Businesses will have to assess it from their perspective and market scenarios and accordingly plan their preparatory strategies*

Fig: 9.1: Five prominent forces shaping the new emerging world

1. De-dollarization: Adapting to Currency Shifts in Global Markets

De-dollarization refers to the reduction of reliance on the US dollar in international transactions, driven by geopolitical tensions, economic shifts, and efforts to diversify currency reserves.

For businesses engaged in international trade, fluctuations in currency exchange rates can lead to increased costs and financial volatility. Supply chains may also be affected, as sourcing materials and components from different countries becomes more complex.

Preparation Strategies:

- Diversify currency holdings and hedge currency risks through financial instruments such as forward contracts and options.
- Develop flexible supply chain strategies that minimize dependencies on specific regions or currencies.
- Monitor geopolitical developments closely and assess potential risks to business operations.
- Cultivate relationships with local partners and authorities to navigate currency-related challenges effectively.

2. **Deglobalization: Navigating Trade Barriers and Market Uncertainty**

Deglobalization, characterized by the retreat from global trade and investment integration, can disrupt established supply chains and market access strategies.

Various tariffs, trade barriers, and geopolitical tensions contribute to market uncertainty and constrain growth opportunities for businesses operating in global markets.

Preparation Strategies:

- Assess exposure to deglobalization risks and develop contingency plans to mitigate disruptions.
- Diversify market presence and localize production facilities to reduce dependence on specific regions.
- Forge strategic partnerships with local suppliers and distributors to enhance supply chain resilience.
- Invest in technology to streamline operations and enhance efficiency, mitigating the impact of deglobalization on costs and competitiveness.

3. **Artificial Intelligence (AI): Embracing Innovation while Navigating Challenges**

The rise of AI and automation presents both opportunities and challenges for businesses across industries. *While AI can improve operational efficiency, enhance customer experiences, and unlock new growth opportunities, it also raises concerns about job displacement, workforce transformation, and ethical implications.*

Preparation Strategies:

- Invest in workforce training and reskilling initiatives to equip employees with skills relevant to the digital economy.
- Foster a culture of continuous learning and innovation to adapt to technological disruptions.
- Prioritize data privacy and ethical AI practices to build trust with customers and stakeholders.
- Collaborate with industry partners and academia to stay abreast of AI advancements and identify opportunities for collaboration.

4. **Rise in Global Conflicts: Mitigating Risks in a Volatile World**

Escalating geopolitical tensions and global conflicts pose significant risks to businesses, including market volatility, supply chain disruptions, and regulatory uncertainty.

Trade restrictions, sanctions, and political instability can impede business operations and erode investor confidence.

Preparation Strategies:

- Conduct geopolitical risk assessments to identify potential threats to business operations.
- Develop robust contingency plans and diversify supply chains to mitigate the impact of geopolitical uncertainties.
- Maintain open lines of communication with stakeholders and engage in diplomatic efforts to mitigate conflict risks.
- Monitor geopolitical developments closely and adapt business strategies accordingly to navigate challenges effectively.

5. Population Dynamics: Adapting to Changing Demographics and Preferences

Shifting demographics – viz., aging populations, urbanization, migration trends, and falling fertility rates in some countries - can have profound implications for consumer preferences, labour markets, and economic growth patterns.

Businesses must adapt to these changing demographic trends to remain relevant and competitive in evolving markets.

Preparation Strategies:

- Conduct demographic analysis to understand the evolving needs and preferences of target demographics.
- Develop tailored products and services to meet the demands of diverse consumer segments.
- Expand into new geographic markets and invest in workforce diversity and inclusion initiatives.
- Foster partnerships with local communities and stakeholders to capitalize on emerging opportunities and address societal challenges.

Conclusion: Prepare for global risk factors

Proactive preparedness is essential for businesses to navigate the uncertainties posed by key global factors effectively. By understanding the potential implications of de-dollarization, deglobalization, artificial Intelligence, global conflicts, falling fertility rates in countries, and population dynamics, organizations can develop robust strategies to mitigate risks, seize opportunities, and thrive.

Embracing a holistic approach to strategic planning and risk management will position businesses to navigate challenges with resilience and agility, ensuring long-term success in a dynamic and interconnected world.

10

Tools & Techniques for Effective Problem Finding

Employing the right tools and techniques is crucial for uncovering insights, generating innovative ideas, and navigating complex challenges. From navigating technological disruptions to addressing shifting consumer demands, organizations face a multitude of challenges that require keen problem-finding skills.

At the heart of problem finding lies a delicate balance between analytical rigor and creative exploration. In today's data-driven world, organizations have access to vast amounts of information, yet extracting meaningful insights requires creative analytical approaches, tools, and methodologies.

In this chapter, we will explore how organizations can leverage data analysis, mind mapping and brainstorming to uncover hidden patterns, identify emerging trends, and generate innovative solutions.

But problem finding is not merely a technical endeavor—it's also a deep human pursuit. Creativity and collaboration play a vital role in the process, as teams come together to explore new ideas, challenge assumptions, and push the boundaries of what's possible. By fostering a culture of creativity and experimentation, organizations can unlock new perspectives, inspire breakthrough innovations, and drive meaningful change.

Therefore, in addition to analytical and creative tools, we'll also delve into the importance of implementing a systematic approach to problem finding. Frameworks and models provide a structured approach for organizing thoughts, analyzing data, and making informed decisions. Whether it's SWOT analysis or PESTEL analysis, these frameworks offer valuable guidance for navigating complex challenges and identifying strategic opportunities.

Furthermore, continuous learning and adaptation also plays a critical role. In a world characterized by constant change and uncertainty, organizations must stay agile and responsive to emerging trends and market shifts.

A. Analytical and Creative Tools

Analytical and creative tools serve as catalysts for uncovering insights and generating novel solutions to complex problems. Let's explore some of the key tools in this category:

Data analysis

Data analysis involves examining datasets to identify trends, connect silo data with a purpose, uncover patterns, and find correlations that can influence decision-making.

Techniques such as descriptive statistics, regression analysis, and data visualization help sift large volumes of data into actionable insights. However, it's essential to recognize that data analysis is not just about delivering reports or creating visually appealing charts—it's about asking the right questions and challenging assumptions to uncover meaningful insights.

Methodology :

- Start with a clear understanding of the purpose behind the analysis and define the problem statement.
- Collect relevant data from internal and external sources, ensuring data quality and completeness.
- Clean and pre-process data to remove inconsistencies and errors, ensuring accuracy and reliability.
- Apply statistical techniques and visualization tools to uncover insights, using creativity to challenge assumptions and explore new perspectives.
- Interpret findings with a critical eye, translating them into actionable recommendations that align with organizational goals and priorities.

By integrating creativity into the data analysis process, analysts can challenge the status quo, explore unconventional approaches, and uncover hidden patterns that may not be apparent through traditional analysis methods. It helps businesses gain a competitive edge and drive innovation in their decision-making processes.

Mind Mapping

Mind mapping is a visual technique for organizing ideas and concepts in a hierarchical structure. By starting with a central theme and branching out into related topics, individuals and teams can explore connections, brainstorm solutions, and identify potential areas for further investigation.

Mind maps facilitate creative thinking, encourage collaboration, and provide a structured framework for problem-solving.

Methodology:

- Define the problem or topic to be explored.
- Brainstorm key ideas and concepts related to the problem. Use McKinsey's MECE (Mutually Exclusive Collectively Exhaustive) technique. This will ensure greater accuracy to the process.
- Organize ideas into categories and subcategories using visual elements. Use the mind mapping schematic approach.

- Continuously refine and expand the mind map as new insights emerge.

Brainstorming

Brainstorming is a collaborative technique for generating a diverse range of ideas in a short amount of time.

Participants are encouraged to suspend judgment and freely express their thoughts, allowing for the exploration of unconventional solutions and innovative approaches.

Methodology:

- Define the problem statement or that challenge that needs to be addressed. It is at this stage that all guns must be fully focussed. Take ample time to ensure there is clarity in the definition and all stakeholders buy into the problem definition.
- Establish ground rules for the brainstorming session, such as encouraging all ideas, deferring judgment, and building on each other's ideas.
- *Use facilitation techniques, such as mind mapping or sticky notes, to capture and organize ideas. You can use the Canvas® technique or the One Page Communication® (OPC) technique as well*
- Encourage active participation and ensure that all voices are heard.

By fostering creativity and promoting open communication, brainstorming sessions can spark breakthrough ideas and drive problem-solving efforts forward. Afterall no idea is a bad idea, and all ideas need not be complete. Every idea is a trigger.

B. Implementing a Systematic Approach

Implementing a systematic approach to problem finding provides structure and guidance for navigating complex challenges. Let's explore some frameworks and models commonly used in this context:

Frameworks and Models for Problem Finding: Various frameworks and models exist to guide problem-finding processes, each offering a unique perspective and approach.

Examples include:

- *SWOT analysis (Strengths, Weaknesses, Opportunities, Threats)*
- *PESTEL analysis (Political, Economic, Social, Technological, Envirnomental, Legal),*
- *The Five Why's technique.*

These frameworks help organizations systematically identify and analyze key factors influencing a problem or opportunity, enabling informed decision-making and strategic planning.

Steps to Follow:

- Select the appropriate framework or model based on the nature of the problem or challenge.
- Gather relevant data and information. *(Refer to Chapter 9 section A for detailed information on the crucial role of PESTEL in strategic adaptation)*
- Apply the framework systematically, considering each factor or dimension in detail.
- Interpret the findings and develop actionable insights and recommendations.

Analysis of Effective Implementation cases:

- Examining real-world case examples of effective problem-finding achievement will provide valuable insights into best practices and success factors.
- By studying how leading organizations have applied frameworks and models to address complex challenges, you can gain inspiration and learn from both their successes and failures.
- Case studies offer practical lessons and actionable takeaways for implementing problem-finding strategies in diverse contexts.

Steps to Follow:

- Research and identify relevant case studies in the industry or domain of interest.
- Analyze the key factors contributing to the success or failure of the problem-finding process.
- Extract lessons learned and the best practices that can be applied to similar situations.
- Adapt and tailor strategies based on the specific needs and context of the organization.

C. Continuous Learning and Adaptation

Continuous learning and adaptation are essential for staying ahead in the curve. Let's explore strategies for being in the forefront and embracing the change:

Keeping Up with Trends and Innovations:

Staying abreast of emerging trends and innovations is critical for driving innovation and maintaining competitiveness.

Organizations can leverage various sources of information, such as industry reports, market research, and professional networks, to monitor trends and identify opportunities for innovation.

By fostering a culture of curiosity and continuous learning, businesses can adapt to evolving market dynamics and seize new growth opportunities.

Steps to Follow:

- Allocate dedicated resources for monitoring industry trends and market developments.
- Establish partnerships with industry experts, research organizations, and academic institutions.
- Engage with speakers from other industries to share their knowledge and expertise and explore cross pollination of ideas and best practices
- Encourage employees to participate in training programs, conferences, and workshops.
- Foster cross-functional collaboration and knowledge sharing to leverage diverse perspectives and insights.

Embracing Change and Uncertainty:

Embracing change and uncertainty is essential for fostering resilience and agility in the dynamic business environment. By cultivating a growth mindset and embracing experimentation, organizations can navigate uncertainty with confidence and adapt to changing circumstances.

Leaders play a crucial role in championing a culture of adaptability and empowering teams to embrace change as an opportunity for growth and innovation.

Steps to Follow:

- Communicate openly and transparently about the need for change and the importance of adaptation.
- Provide resources and support for employees to experiment, take calculated risks, and learn from failure.
- Foster a culture of flexibility and agility, where teams can quickly pivot and adjust to changing priorities and circumstances.
- Celebrate successes and milestones, reinforcing the value of adaptability and resilience in achieving organizational goals.

Conclusion: Unlock potential through analytical and creative techniques

Mastering the tools and techniques for effective problem finding is essential for driving innovation, navigating complexity, and leading the game in current competitive business landscape. By embracing analytical and creative approaches, implementing systematic frameworks, and fostering a culture of continuous learning and adaptation, organizations can unlock new opportunities, foresee risks, solve potential challenges ahead, and achieve sustainable growth in the digital age.

11

The Role of Diversity in Problem Finding

Diversity of Thought and Experience

The convergence of individuals possessing varied backgrounds, experiences, and perspectives instigates a confluence of questions that ultimately foster innovation and progress. Therefore, diversity is crucial for the expansion and success of an organisation. Diversity of perspectives ignites a transformative process in the dynamic problem finding exercise, during which the very nature of the inquiry changes.

This phenomenon, often referred to as "changing the question," becomes a natural outcome of embracing diversity. In this chapter, we explore how diversity not only enriches finding but also leads to a periodic re-evaluation and reframing of the questions we ask.

Through examining case studies, strategies, and illustrations, we uncover the profound impact of this approach on fostering inclusive teams, global perspectives, and ultimately, innovative solutions.

Importance of Varied Perspectives

In the realm of problem finding, diversity acts as a catalyst for change, offering a fresh lens through which to view challenges and opportunities. One of the most potent tools in problem finding is the ability to "change the question." When faced with a problem, individuals often default to asking familiar questions rooted in their existing knowledge and experiences.

However, by consciously shifting the focus and reframing the question, they can unlock new perspectives and unearth innovative solutions.

Consider a team grappling with declining sales figures for a product. Instead of asking, "How can we increase sales?" they might reframe the question to, "What unmet needs are we failing to address in our target market?" This subtle shift in perspective opens up a wealth of possibilities, encouraging the team to explore alternative approaches and challenge conventional assumptions.

Case Studies Showing the Impact of Diversity

Numerous case studies underscore the transformative power of changing the question in problem finding. Take, for instance, the story of a struggling *retail chain* seeking to revitalize its business model. Conventional wisdom dictated that the company should focus on slashing prices and increasing advertising spend. However, by challenging this premise and reframing the question to, "How can we redefine the retail experience for the modern consumer?" the company embarked on a journey of innovation that ultimately led to its resurgence.

Similarly, a multinational pharmaceutical company faced with stagnating research efforts shifted its focus from developing incremental improvements to existing drugs to reimagining healthcare delivery systems in underserved communities. This change in question not only reignited the company's passion for innovation but also yielded ground-breaking solutions with far-reaching societal impact.

Building Inclusive Teams

Strategies for Creating Diverse Teams

Changing the question extends beyond problem finding to the composition of teams themselves. *Organizations striving to build diverse teams must first challenge conventional hiring practices and broaden their definition of talent.*

Instead of seeking candidates who fit a predetermined mould, they should ask, "What unique perspectives and experiences can each individual bring to the table?"

Promoting diversity in leadership is another essential

strategy for fostering inclusive teams. By appointing leaders who champion diversity and actively seek out dissenting voices, organizations can create an environment where different viewpoints are valued and celebrated.

Overcoming Bias and Encouraging Dialogue

Despite efforts to promote diversity, unconscious bias can still permeate team dynamics and decision-making processes. To counteract this, organizations must cultivate a culture of openness and dialogue, where team members feel empowered to challenge assumptions and voice dissenting opinions. By actively seeking out diverse perspectives and engaging in respectful debate, teams can harness the collective intelligence of their members and drive meaningful change.

Global Perspectives

Learning from Different Cultures and Industries

Transformative change can be instigated by the multitude of insights that global perspectives provide. Organisations can discover innovative solutions that transcend geographical boundaries and obtain fresh perspectives on familiar challenges by conducting research across various industries and cultures.

For example, a technology start-up struggling to gain traction in its home market might look to emerging economies for inspiration. By reframing the question from, "How can we compete with established players?" to, "What unmet needs exist in rapidly growing markets?" the company can identify untapped opportunities and leverage its agility to capture market share.

Leveraging Global Insights for Local Solutions

While global perspectives provide valuable inspiration, it is essential to tailor insights to the local context. What works in one country or industry may not necessarily translate directly to another. Therefore, organizations must approach global insights with a critical eye, adapting and customizing them to address local challenges and meet the needs of diverse stakeholders.

Key takeaways from this exploration include:

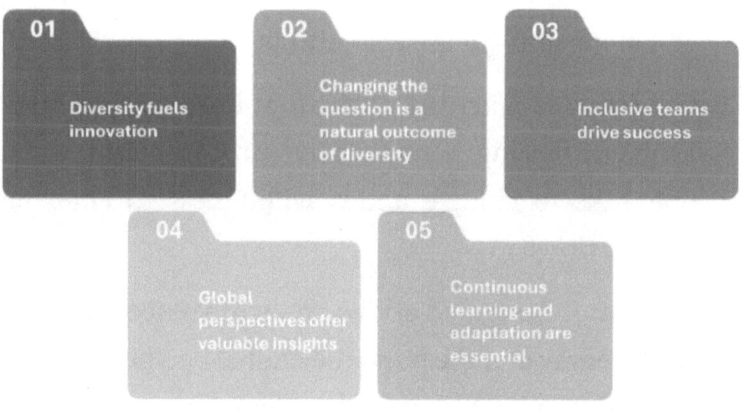

Fig: 11.1: Key Takeaways: Role of diversity in problem finding

1. **Diversity fuels innovation:** Varied perspectives bring forth a variety of questions, fostering creativity and driving the discovery of novel solutions.

2. **Changing the question is a natural outcome of diversity:** Embracing diverse perspectives naturally leads to a periodic re-evaluation and reframing of the questions we ask, opening doors to new insights and opportunities.

3. **Inclusive teams drive success:** Building teams that value and celebrate diversity creates an environment where all voices are heard, leading to better decision-making and more innovative problem finding.

4. **Global perspectives offer** valuable insights: Learning from different cultures and industries enriches problem finding, enabling organizations to leverage global insights for local solutions.

5. **Continuous learning and adaptation are essential:** Problem finding is an iterative process that requires openness to change and a willingness to challenge assumptions.

The outcomes described above are highly encouraging in light of diversity and the pursuit of global perspectives. The implementation of a diverse problem finding approach will yield significant benefits for the organisation.

Conclusion: Power of diversity in problem finding

Diversity and the practice of changing the question are not just strategies; they are guiding principles that drive organizations toward success in the complex and dynamic landscape of problem finding. By adopting these principles, organisations have the ability to generate novel opportunities, foster innovation, and establish a more promising future for all. Organisations can flourish in a dynamic global environment and effectively navigate uncertainty by adopting an open mindset towards diversity and a paradigm of questioning.

12

My Data-Driven Problem Finding Framework

In the midst of an overwhelming amount of information, problem finding emerges as the more formidable task: discerning and articulating the fundamental concerns that propel organisational performance.

This chapter provides an in-depth examination of problem finding, presenting an exhaustive framework that is specifically designed for the purposes of business analysis and data analytics. I strongly believe that organisations can effectively guide strategic decision-making, surmount risks, and uncover latent opportunities by developing proficiency in problem finding.

Kidambi's Data -Driven Problem Finding Framework

At the heart of effective problem finding lies a structured framework comprising four essential components: Data Refinement, Data Organization, Insight Exploration, and Insight Elevation. Let me elaborate these one by one.

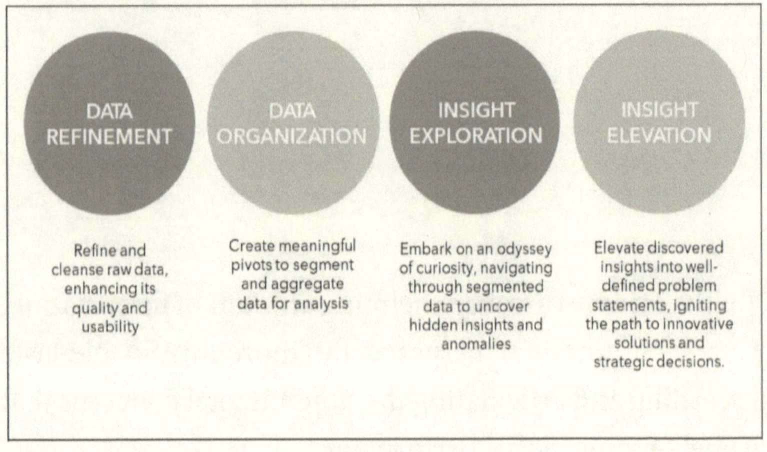

Fig : 12.1 : Kidambi's Data-Driven Problem Finding Framework

Data Refinement:

Data refinement is the foundational step in the problem finding framework, focusing on enhancing the quality and usability of raw data. In this phase, an analyst must meticulously clean and refine the dataset to ensure its accuracy, completeness, and relevance to the problem at hand.

To begin, a comprehensive audit must be conducted of the data, identifying errors, inconsistencies, and missing values. This may involve de-duplication, outlier detection, and data validation techniques to eliminate duplicates and anomalies that could skew the analysis results.

Next, each data field must be refined, ensuring clarity

and consistency in communication. This may entail standardizing data formats, resolving naming conventions, and creating additional columns for contextual information.

Further the analyst should collaborate with stakeholders to establish a "parent database" – a comprehensive repository of all relevant data fields essential for addressing the problem statement. This parent database serves as the foundation for subsequent analysis and decision-making.

By refining the data, the groundwork is laid for accurate analysis and meaningful insights.

A thorough data refinement process ensures that the data is fit for purpose, enabling stakeholders to make informed decisions based on reliable information.

Data Organisation:

Data segmentation plays a pivotal role in organizing and prioritizing data based on key parameters relevant to the problem statement. In this phase, the dataset is segmented into distinct categories or groups to facilitate targeted analysis and exploration.

The segmentation process begins with identifying relevant criteria for grouping the data. Here, at this stage, one must have 'end-in-mind' and must also seek the help of a subject matter expert. Further, collaborating with stakeholders is a must to define segmentation criteria that align with the organization's goals and objectives.

Once the segmentation criteria are established, segmentation techniques are applied to divide the dataset into mutually exclusive and collectively exhaustive segments. This ensures that each data point falls into a distinct category and covers the entire spectrum of the problem domain.

Additionally, the analyst should leverage segmentation tools and methodologies to streamline the segmentation process and ensure consistency across the dataset. Techniques such as clustering, stratification, and cohort analysis help identify patterns and relationships within the data.

By segmenting the data, it is possible to gain deeper insights into specific subgroups or segments, enabling targeted analysis and exploration. *Segmentation enhances the granularity of the analysis, allowing stakeholders to uncover hidden trends, anomalies, and opportunities within the dataset.*

Insight Exploration:

Exploration represents the investigative phase of the problem finding framework, where the analysts delve into segmented data to uncover hidden insights and anomalies. In this phase, the analyst applies curiosity-led critical thinking to challenge assumptions, questions the status quo, and explores non-traditional premises.

Here, the analyst embarks on an OC (Open Curiosity) journey, probing the segmented data with a curious mindset to uncover patterns, trends, and outliers. The analytical techniques such as data visualization, statistical analysis, and predictive modelling are leveraged to explore the dataset from multiple perspectives.

Cross-functional collaboration and diverse perspectives are also encouraged to foster innovative thinking and to uncover novel insights. It gets easier to gain fresh perspectives and unique insights into the data, by engaging stakeholders from different departments and disciplines.

Throughout the exploration process, the analyst remains open-minded and adaptable, embracing uncertainty and ambiguity as opportunities for discovery. Their analysis is refined iteratively, testing hypotheses, and validating findings to ensure robust and reliable results.

By embracing exploration and discovery, organizations can unearth hidden insights and anomalies within the dataset, *paving the way for innovative solutions and strategic decisions. This phase of the problem finding framework fosters creativity, curiosity, and a relentless pursuit of knowledge.*

Insight Elevation:

Elevation marks the culmination of the data-driven problem finding framework, where the analyst translates insights and discoveries into well-defined problem statements and strategic approach. In this phase, the analyst elevates his/her discoveries into tangible outcomes, igniting the path to innovative solutions and transformative change.

The process is initiated by distilling the findings into clear and concise problem statements that articulate the underlying challenges and opportunities uncovered during the exploration phase. These problem statements serve as the foundation for strategic decision-making and action planning.

Next, to develop actionable strategies and initiatives aimed at addressing the identified problems and seizing opportunities, analyst should collaborate with the stakeholders. Then, initiatives are prioritized based on their potential impact, feasibility, and alignment with organizational goals.

Further, storytelling techniques are leveraged to communicate his/her findings and recommendations effectively to key stakeholders. By crafting compelling narratives backed by data-driven insights, analysts inspire action and foster buy-in from decision-makers and influencers.

Throughout the elevation process, the analyst should remain focused on driving tangible outcomes and delivering value to the organization. The implementation of strategic initiatives should be monitored, key performance indicators are tracked, and should follow iteration in their approach, based on feedback and results.

By elevating the discoveries into well-defined problem statements and strategic recommendations, *organizations can empower themselves to drive innovation, optimize performance, and achieve their goals. Elevation represents the culmination of the problem finding process, transforming insights into impact and driving positive change.*

Conclusion: Structured framework for data analytics

Effective problem finding is essential for driving meaningful insights and strategic decisions in business analysis and data analytics. By following a structured framework that emphasizes data refinement, segmentation, exploration, and insight elevation, organizations can unlock hidden opportunities, mitigate risks, and drive innovation. Embracing problem finding as a core component of the analysis process is key to unlocking the full potential of data-driven decision-making.

13

Case Studies in Problem Finding

(Unknown Knowns)

Discovering Unknown Knowns:

In this insightful chapter, we embark on a captivating journey through the real-world challenges encountered by various organizations across different industries.

Each case study presented is not just a narrative; but based on my hands-on experience, I unravelled the complex web of symptomatic issues presented by various corporate houses leading to the discovery of the elusive unknown knowns. The essence of these narratives lies in the understanding that organizations are often aware of what they know yet remain in the dark about what they don't know.

Through diligent and responsible consulting approach I am bridging this gap in knowledge and awareness. The underlying issues that evade the conventional viewing patterns are uncovered by delving deep into the data using my experience as a storyteller of business behaviours and operational nuances. Data analysis, in these contexts, becomes more than a tool; it transforms into a compass that guides through the fog of surface-level symptoms to the core of underlying problems.

Note: This chapter stands out as a unique compilation of live case studies, meticulously curated from various corporate engagements, where a data-driven problem-finding approach illuminated the path to solutions previously shrouded in ambiguity.

Real Life Case Studies:

Each case study reinforces the notion that problem finding is invariably about dissecting the dimensions of 'who,' 'when,' 'where,' 'what,' 'why,' and 'how,' bringing clarity to the complexities that businesses face. *It underscores a fundamental truth: while solutions may often be straightforward, accurately defining the problem is the real challenge.*

This chapter, therefore, is not just a collection of problems solved; it's a chronicle of discovery, insight, and the strategic unveiling of hidden truths through the lens of problem finding.

As we navigate through these live case studies, I not only share my experiences but also explain the meticulous process of identifying problems that lie beneath the layer of symptomatic challenges.

I promise here to enlighten, educate, and inspire, by offering a unique perspective on the transformative power of a problem-finding approach in the consulting realm. Come join me in this explorative journey!

Case Study 1: Turning Losses into Profits for a Technology Distribution Company

Background:

A technology hardware distribution company, with over 30 years in the industry, faced a critical financial challenge. Despite having satisfactory revenue figures, the company was experiencing net profit losses month after month.

The critical *unknown known* to the CEO was the underlying reasons of the teams' inability to meet and surpass operational costs. Operating at a Gross Profit (GP) of 2.7% against an operational cost of 4.8% of total revenue, the main issue was clear: profitability was in jeopardy.

> *"Uncovering the 'unknown knowns' in business is not just about data analysis; it's about embracing curiosity to shift focus from volume to value, transforming challenges into opportunities for sustained profitability."*

Challenge:

The CEO, aware of the symptomatic problems but unable to pinpoint the underlying issues, sought external expertise to identify and address the root causes of the continuous losses. The task was to uncover the " unknown knowns" that were hindering profitability despite the company's long-standing presence in the market.

Approach:

Embracing a *curiosity-led problem-finding approach*, an exhaustive analysis of the company's operational data was conducted, including sales, receivables, and inventory data.

The investigation focused on the company's business model, particularly its reliance on large-scale, low-margin category sales, which, while contributing significantly to the top line, were detrimental to overall profitability due to associated receivable risks and resource allocation.

Solution:

The analysis revealed that the company's strategy of chasing top-line growth at the expense of bottom-line impact was unsustainable. The key to turning around the situation was to shift focus from low-margin items to medium and high-margin products.

Despite initial resistance, the management and operating teams were guided to understand the detrimental effects of low-margin sales and the benefits of prioritizing higher-margin business segments, such as Microsoft Surface, Apple products, and PC accessories.

Outcome:

The strategic shift to higher-margin offerings significantly improved the company's financial health.

The Gross Profit margin increased from a precarious 2.7% to a healthy 5.6%, marking the transition from operating at a loss to achieving profitability.

Over the subsequent three years, the company's GP margin further rose to 8.5%, demonstrating sustained improvement and a successful turnaround.

Case Study 1: One Page Summary

1. Background: A technology distribution company with 30 years in the market faced consistent net profit losses for over 16 months, despite adequate revenue, due to a Gross Profit (GP) of 2.7% against operational costs of 4.8%.	**2. Challenge:** The CEO sought external help to identify the underlying causes of the losses, aiming to uncover the "unknown knowns" affecting profitability.
3. Approach: A curiosity-led problem-finding analysis of operational data was conducted, revealing the company's unsustainable focus on low-margin, high-volume sales.	**4. Solution:** The company shifted its strategy to emphasize medium and high-margin products, overcoming initial resistance to prioritize more profitable business segments.
5. Outcome: This strategic pivot increased the GP margin from 2.7% to 5.6%, eventually reaching 8.5% over three years, successfully reversing the company's financial trajectory towards sustained profitability.	

Case Study 2: Revitalizing Profit Margins in Traditional High-ticket Jewellery Sales

Background:

A renowned jeweller, cherished for its fine jewellery and solitaire diamonds, encountered a perplexing challenge: the erosion of net profits despite robust sales. Habitual deep discounting, often reaching 50% to 70%, became the norm, with sales personnel frequently soliciting the owner for approval on these cuts. This practice led to a scenario where despite high ticket sales, averaging above $80,000, profitability was compromised, illustrating a critical *unknown knowns* in their sales strategy.

Challenge:

The jeweller's primary issue was the detrimental impact of habitual discounting on profitability. The sales team's reliance on significant price reductions to close sales was a symptomatic problem, but the underlying unknown known was the lack of understanding across the organization about the true cost of these discounts on the company's bottom line.

Approach:

Employing a *curiosity-led problem finding approach*, a comprehensive analysis of the company's sales data was undertaken to unearth the hidden patterns and consequences of the prevailing discount culture. This approach revealed the significant impact of even a 1% discount on overall profitability and highlighted a lack of incentive alignment and accountability among the sales team. The analysis showed that bonuses were awarded at the owner's discretion, leading to a culture where sales personnel were not motivated to maintain pricing integrity.

Solution:

"Unlock the power of one percent: small changes in pricing strategy can yield significant results. Shift your focus from deep discounts to incremental value and witness the transformative impact on profitability"

The intervention focused on recalibrating the sales team's understanding of discounts' impact through educational sessions emphasizing the "power of one percent." A restructured incentive system was introduced to align sales efforts with preserving profit margins. This system made a clear distinction between earned incentives and discretionary bonuses, shifting towards a model that rewarded sales personnel quarterly for achieving sales without resorting to excessive discounting. This initiative aimed to foster a culture of accountability and pride in earning incentives through performance.

Outcome:

Despite initial resistance and doubts about the new incentive program's credibility, the shift in strategy yielded remarkable results. The sales team, motivated by the new rewards system, adjusted their sales tactics, leading to an impressive increase in net profits by 5.1 million dirhams ($1.4 million USD) by year-end, without an increase in revenue. This case highlighted the discovery and resolution of an unknown known— the unacknowledged financial drain caused by indiscriminate discounting and the transformative power of aligning sales incentives with company profitability.

Case Study 2: One Page Summary

1. Background: Despite high sales, deep discounting was eroding a jeweler's net profits, with a lack of understanding of the discounts' true cost.	**2. Challenge:** The main issue lay in habitual discounting's negative impact on profitability.
3. Approach: Employing a curiosity-led problem-finding analysis, the sales team's data revealed the profound impact of even a 1% discount and a misaligned incentive system	**4. Solution:** The sales team's perception of discounts was recalibrated through educational initiatives and a new incentive system that rewarded achieving sales targets without excessive discounts
5. Outcome: The new strategy overcame initial resistance and significantly improved net profits by $1.4 million USD by year-end, demonstrating the power of aligning sales incentives with profitability.	

Case Study 3: Transforming Financial Performance - From Leakages to Gains for a Distribution Company

Background:

The case centers on a distribution company specializing in selling tyres imported from factories worldwide. Despite maintaining a healthy gross profit (GP), the company faced a perplexing issue: a significantly lower net profit leading to reluctance in paying bonuses to employees. Despite the team's commendable performance and achieving a healthier GP, the discrepancy in net profit puzzled the top management.

Challenge:

The challenge lay in understanding why the net profit lagged behind expectations despite a healthy GP. The discrepancy raised concerns about the company's financial health and threatened employee morale due to the inability to pay bonuses.

"Embrace the unknown knowns. By challenging the status quo and nurturing curiosity, we uncover hidden inefficiencies, driving financial resilience and fostering growth"

Approach:

To tackle the challenge, a well-structured problem-finding approach was adopted, leveraging the "Start with Why" methodology. They began by scrutinizing the company's Profit and Loss (P&L) statement, aiming to uncover underlying issues in cost management.

By meticulously analyzing each expense and questioning its necessity, the team sought to identify inefficiencies contributing to the lower net profit.

Solution:

During the analysis, a significant discrepancy in bank charges drew the attention of the curiosity-led mind, which accounted for a staggering 3.8% of the company's revenue. Different sets of silo data were analysed and connected meaningfully. Such analysis revealed that the company was unnecessarily trading import documents with the bank for a 270-day period, resulting in inflated interest costs.

Armed with this insight, renegotiating bank documents for a reduced period of 240 days was recommended, thereby slashing interest costs and improving the company's net profit.

Outcome:

Implementing the recommended solution led to a

remarkable turnaround in the company's financial performance.

By optimizing the importation process and negotiating shorter bank document periods, the company achieved a substantial reduction in interest costs. This, in turn, bolstered the net profit, enabling the company to enhance financial stability and allocate funds towards rewarding employee performance.

The successful identification and rectification of this single inefficiency underscored the power of strategic problem-finding and optimization in driving financial resilience and growth.

Case Study 3: One Page Summary

1. Background: A tire distribution company faced a puzzling issue: despite a healthy gross profit (GP), net profit remained significantly lower, impacting bonus payouts.

2. Challenge: Understanding why net profit lagged despite a healthy GP raised concerns about financial health and employee morale

3. Approach: Using the "Start with Why" methodology, the Profit and Loss statement was scrutinized, uncovering inefficiencies in cost management

4. Solution: Identifying a significant bank charge discrepancy of 3.8% of revenue, the team recommended negotiating bank documents for a reduced 240-day period, cutting interest costs. This was possible after connecting various silo data.

5. Outcome: Implementing the solution led to a remarkable turnaround, reducing interest costs, and bolstering net profit, enhancing financial stability, and enabling rewards for employee performance.

Case Study 4: From Oversight to Opportunity: Operational Optimization in a Facility Management Company

Background:

A leading facility management company made a longstanding decision to lease their fleet vehicles without questioning its validity. Despite the fleet growing to over 40 vehicles, the lease arrangement continued unquestioned, highlighting a significant unknown known within the company's operational strategy.

Challenge:

The challenge was rooted in the company's adherence to the status quo, with the lease decision becoming a routine practice without scrutiny.

The failure to challenge this decision resulted in missed opportunities and overlooked cost-saving alternatives.

Approach:

In a bid to unearth hidden inefficiencies and challenge the lease arrangement, a curiosity-driven problem-finding approach was employed. This led to questioning the status quo and carrying out a complete analysis to validate the status-quo biased decision. Hence, a thorough analysis comparing the benefits of leasing versus purchasing the fleet vehicles, considering factors such as cash outflow, branding opportunities, and long-term cost implications, was performed

Solution:

The analysis revealed a substantial financial benefit of approximately $350,000 by opting to purchase the vehicles instead of leasing. Additionally, owning the vehicles allowed the company to leverage branding opportunities, with an estimated branding value of $950,000.

By weighing the cash outflow, insurance costs, registration fees, and other associated expenses, transitioning from leasing to purchasing the fleet of vehicles was recommended

Outcome:

Implementing the solution resulted in significant cost savings (USD 350K) and branding opportunities (USD 950K) for the facility management company. By owning the fleet vehicles, they not only reduced their cash outflow but also enhanced their brand visibility and market presence.

"From overlooked oversights to seizing opportunities, strategic problem-finding drives operational optimization and financial success"

The decision to challenge the lease arrangement and explore alternative options demonstrated the power of strategic problem-finding in driving operational efficiency and financial success.

Case Study 4: One Page Summary

1. Background: A leading facility management company continued leasing their fleet vehicles, overlooking its validity as the fleet grew to over 40 vehicles, highlighting a significant operational oversight	**2. Challenge:** Adherence to the status quo led to missed cost-saving opportunities, as the company failed to challenge the lease decision, resulting in overlooked efficiencies and financial gains
3. Approach: Using a curiosity-driven approach, a comparison study between leasing and purchasing fleet vehicles was carried out. Further others costs and branding opportunities were carried out to uncover hidden inefficiencies	**4. Solution:** Analysis revealed a $350K benefit in purchasing over leasing, with ownership offering a $950K branding opportunity. Transitioning to vehicle ownership was recommended for cost reduction and enhanced brand visibility.

5. Outcome: Implementing the solution led to $350K in cost savings and a $950K branding opportunity. Owning the fleet enhanced market presence and operational efficiency, showcasing the power of strategic problem-finding.

Case Study 5: Unveiling the Language Discrepancy for a Real Estate Firm

Background:

A prominent real estate firm encountered a puzzling trend – a significant portion of their bookings were being cancelled, sparking concern among stakeholders. Initial analysis revealed a cancellation rate of approximately 23%, prompting questions about customer satisfaction and operational efficiency. Given the high cost of customer acquisition and the potential revenue implications of booking losses, addressing this issue became imperative.

Challenge:

The challenge faced by the real estate firm was the right understanding of the root cause for the high cancellation rate. The staggering figure was accepted as 'normal' especially in an upward price trending market, this was beneficial too. However, it could prove extremely expensive in a downtrend market condition

Approach:

Traditional analysis failed to prompt human action. A deep, granular-level analysis was carried out to explore what was missing and to draw attention, thus leading to human action. The known aspect was the high percentage of booking loss. What remained unknown was how to produce a convincing and factual analysis that would result in the right action. Despite identifying the issue, the indiscriminate use of the term "cancellation" obscured the distinction between customer-initiated cancellations and seller-driven disqualifications. This inconsistency in language hindered accurate analysis, making it crucial to refine the data and clarify the classification of cancellations.

Refining the data ensured the correct attribution for booking loss, enabling a different set of strategic activities to monitor and minimize booking loss.

Solution:

Armed with this insight, the team rectified the language discrepancy, clarified the distinction between customer cancellations and seller disqualifications, and implemented measures to reduce booking cancellations. This included deploying strategies to enhance customer satisfaction and trust in the firm's services.

"In the realm of business analysis, clarity of language is paramount. Clarity of language uncovers hidden opportunities and drives strategic decision-making"

Outcome:

The outcome of the solution was significant. By refining the data and segmenting it appropriately, the real estate firm was able to curtail booking losses and improve operational efficiency. Considering the average ticket size of the property at USD 450,000, a 1% reduction in booking losses accounted for 45 bookings annually. Therefore, every 1% improvement in booking loss curtailment represented an approximate loss of revenue of USD 20 million. The deployment of the appropriate strategy yielded a 1.5% reduction in booking loss immediately, drawing enhanced management attention to the issue and demonstrating the impact of problem finding in driving strategic decision-making. Additionally, the potential revenue implications of booking losses underscored the importance of addressing this issue promptly and effectively.

Case Study 5: One Page Summary

1. Background: A real estate firm faced a cancellation rate of approximately 23%, which raised questions about customer satisfaction and operational efficiency, given the high cost of customer acquisition.	**2. Challenge:** Understanding the root cause of the high cancellation rate was crucial. While seemingly 'normal' in an upward-trending market, it could be costly in a downturn. Traditional analysis failed to prompt action, necessitating a deeper, granular-level analysis.
3. Approach: A meticulous problem-finding approach was employed. Refining data and clarifying cancellation classifications became imperative for accurate attribution and effective strategic activities.	**4. Solution:** The team rectified language discrepancies, clarifying customer cancellations versus seller disqualifications, and implemented measures to reduce cancellations. Strategies were deployed to enhance customer satisfaction and trust.
5. Outcome: Refining and segmenting the data curtailed booking losses and improved operational efficiency. With the average property ticket size at USD 450,000, a 1% reduction in booking losses represented an approximate revenue loss of USD 20 million annually. Immediate deployment of strategies led to a 1.5% reduction in booking loss, highlighting the impact of problem finding in decision-making.	

Case Study 6: Navigating Uncomfortable Realities in a Trading & Distribution company

Background:

In a financially robust trading & distribution company, with revenues exceeding $100 million and positive financial indicators across the board, the CEO sensed an underlying discomfort within the organization. Despite the outward appearance of success, a sense of unease persisted, prompting a deeper investigation into the unseen aspects of the business.

Challenge:

The challenge lay in uncovering the unknown knowns – those hidden realities lurking beneath the surface of apparent success. Despite no red flags raised by the CFO, the CEO's intuition urged further exploration. With a wealth of data available within the ERP system, the team embarked on a journey to decipher the enigma that shrouded the company's operations.

Approach:

Driven by curiosity and a thirst for insight, the team delved into the transactional data, seeking to connect disparate pieces of information. The analysis revealed startling revelations: 96% of the business was attributed to a single brand, 98% to one product segment, and more than half of the business stemmed from just six customers. Additionally, a staggering 80% of the business was generated by a single salesperson. This concentration of risk highlighted the need for immediate action to mitigate potential vulnerabilities.

Solution:

Recognizing the imperative for change, the team identified risk mitigation as the primary priority. A shift in both the line and manner of conducting business was deemed necessary. The solution entailed diversifying the brand portfolio and expanding into adjacent product lines. Over a three-year period, the company strategically reduced its dependency on the dominant brand, diversifying its revenue streams and mitigating risk.

"In times of comfort and complacency, it is the willingness to confront the unknown that distinguishes true leaders from the rest"

Outcome:

The proactive approach to problem-solving yielded transformative results. By addressing the underlying risk factors and embracing strategic diversification, the company not only reduced its dependency on a single brand but also experienced exponential revenue growth, surpassing the $300 million mark. This strategic shift, guided by a curiosity-led problem-finding approach, propelled the organization into a new era of sustainable growth and resilience.

Case Study 6: One Page Summary

1. Background: In a financially sound trading distribution company, with revenues exceeding $100 million, a sense of discomfort spurred a deeper investigation into unseen business aspects.

2. Challenge: Despite outward success, hidden realities lurked beneath the surface, prompting the need to decipher unknown knowns and mitigate potential risks.

3. Approach: Driven by curiosity, transactional data analysis revealed alarming concentrations of risk: 96% of business from one brand, 98% from a single product segment, and 80% by one salesperson.

4. Solution: Driven by curiosity, transactional data analysis revealed alarming concentrations of risk: 96% of business from one brand, 98% from a single product segment, and 80% by one salesperson.

5. Outcome: The proactive approach yielded transformative results, reducing dependency on a single brand and surpassing $300 million in revenue, marking a new era of growth and resilience.

Case Study 7: Priority Reassessment: Unveiling Operational Blind Spots in Services Industry

Background:

In the services industry, the task of setting priorities for work orders is crucial for efficient operations. However, encountered scenarios with complex priority levels, ranging from P1 to P9, and in some cases, only three levels (P1, P2, P3), highlighted the need for a strategic approach to priority setting.

Challenge:

Despite outward efficiency, operational decisions were often made hastily, resulting in misclassified priorities and knee-jerk reactions. The lack of a strategic perspective led to the misattribution of priorities, with critical tasks often categorized as lower priorities.

Approach:

Driven by curiosity, a thorough analysis of priority setting processes revealed discrepancies in how priorities were assigned. Despite surface-level efficiency metrics, deeper scrutiny uncovered the true nature of operational challenges.

Solution:

Recognizing the need for strategic oversight, priority setting processes were revisited and redesigned. Operational tasks were appropriately prioritized based on their impact and urgency, with management involvement mandated to ensure alignment with organizational goals.

"In the realm of operations, strategic prioritization is the cornerstone of efficiency and success"

Outcome:

The revised priority setting approach led to a significant improvement in operational effectiveness and customer satisfaction. By accurately prioritizing tasks, the facility management company was able to address critical issues promptly, leading to enhanced customer happiness and overall operational performance.

Case Study 7: One Page Summary

1. Background: Facility management companies often face challenges in setting priorities for work orders. Complex priority levels, ranging from P1 to P9 or just three levels (P1, P2, P3), underscored the need for a strategic approach to priority setting.	**2. Challenge:** Despite surface-level efficiency, operational decisions were marred by hastily assigned priorities, leading to misclassification and knee-jerk reactions. The absence of a strategic perspective exacerbated operational inefficiencies.
3. Approach: A curiosity-driven analysis uncovered discrepancies in priority assignment processes. Despite apparent efficiency metrics, deeper scrutiny revealed operational challenges lurking beneath the surface.	**4. Solution:** Realizing the importance of strategic oversight, priority setting processes were overhauled. Tasks were prioritized based on impact and urgency, with mandatory management involvement ensuring alignment with organizational objectives.
5. Outcome: The revamped priority setting approach significantly enhanced operational effectiveness and customer satisfaction. Accurate prioritization enabled prompt resolution of critical issues, resulting in heightened customer happiness and overall operational performance.	

14

Embracing the Art of Problem Finding

We have come to the end of our enlightening journey through this book "The Art of Problem Finding," so let us take a moment to reflect on the important lessons and insights we have gained. I set out to uncover more about the "unknown knowns" and "unknown unknowns" in today's corporate world and demonstrate how crucial this knowledge is for tackling the problems that modern firms encounter throughout this book. Innovation, growth, and resilience necessitate the ability to anticipate and prevent problems before they even arise.

Reflecting on the Journey through the Book

From the initial chapters, which laid the groundwork on the importance of problem finding, to the insightful case studies that provided real-world applications, each page has served to highlight the transformative power of this skill.

This book also showed the cognitive biases that can cloud our judgments and how fostering intellectual curiosity can lead to breakthroughs even in the most established industries.

Looking Forward: The Future of Problem Finding in Business and Society

With the certain knowledge that new challenges and opportunities will undoubtedly emerge in the future, problem finding expertise will undoubtedly grow in importance, as I foresee. Businesses that are able to predict and manoeuvre through these transformations will not only endure but prosper as technologies and societies progress. They will have a significant impact on society by fostering an environment that appreciates innovation, foresight, and the ongoing quest for progress.

Call to Action for Readers

Hence, the time to act is now. I encourage you all to take the insights from this book and apply them within your organizations and daily lives. I call the readers of this book to take action to bring change.

Cultivate environments where questioning the status quo is the norm, where data is not just collected but analyzed with a discerning eye, and where every employee feels empowered to share their observations and ideas.

To prioritize these call-to-action points based on their criticality - in fostering a problem-finding culture and their impact on innovation and growth within a corporate environment – I categorized them into "Top 10" for foundational actions and "Next 5" for advanced strategies.

Note: This segmentation is guided by the immediate versus long-term benefits and the general applicability across various organizational levels and industries.

Top 10 Call to Action points (Foundational):

1. Cultivate Curiosity: Essential for fostering an environment where problem finding becomes second nature.
2. Foster Open Communication: Crucial for ensuring that ideas and observations are freely shared.
3. Promote Diverse Perspectives: Diversity drives innovation by bringing different viewpoints to the table.
4. Engage in Active Listening: A fundamental skill for uncovering hidden problems and understanding complex issues.
5. Challenge Cognitive Biases: Directly impacts the quality of decision-making and problem identification.
6. Utilize Data Effectively: The backbone of modern problem finding, enabling evidence-based insights.
7. Adopt a Growth Mindset: Encourages resilience and adaptability, key traits for navigating uncertainties.
8. Stay Informed on Industry Trends: Ensures that the

organization remains competitive and proactive.

9. Practice Scenario Planning: Prepares the organization for future uncertainties by anticipating possible challenges.

10. Share Knowledge and Insights: Amplifies the impact of problem finding by leveraging collective intelligence.

Next 5: (For Advanced Strategies)

1. Implement Regular Review Sessions: Important for continuous improvement but requires an established culture of feedback.

2. Encourage Risk-taking: Vital for innovation but needs a supportive environment to truly be effective.

3. Reward Innovation: Critical for sustaining motivation but follows the establishment of a clear innovation framework.

4. Reflect on Failures: Offers deep learning opportunities but is most beneficial in a mature culture that values transparency.

5. Invest in Continuous Education: Supports long-term growth and adaptation but depends on the foundational belief in continuous development.

Final Words

As we close this chapter and the book, remember that problem finding is a journey without end. It is an ongoing quest that requires persistence, adaptability, and a willingness to continually learn. With the art of problem finding as your compass, you are now equipped to embark on this journey, to lead with vision and purpose, and to make a lasting impact on the world of business and beyond.

Embrace the challenges ahead by implementing the strategies and techniques shared within these pages. Engage with your teams, leverage your data, and most importantly, remain endlessly curious about the problems that have yet to be discovered.

Let 'The Art of Problem Finding' be your guide to not only identifying the challenges of tomorrow but also creating the solutions that will define the future.

Thank you for joining me on this adventure. Now, go forth and find those problems—because within them lies the seeds of your next great opportunity.

***

Notes

Notes

Notes

References:

1. Team, E. S. (2024, January 5). The Role of Curiosity in Personal and Professional Growth - ESS Global Training Solutions. ESS Global Training Solutions.

   https://esoftskills.com/the-role-of-curiosity-in-personal-and-professional-growth/

2. Why Cultivating A Curious Mindset Is Essential For Entrepreneurs https://fastercapital.com/topics/why-cultivating-a-curious-mindset-is-essential-for-entrepreneurs.html

3. The Significance of AI and HI: A Symbiotic Relationship

   https://www.linkedin.com/pulse/significance-ai-hi-symbiotic-relationship-darren-richard-hngue

4. Rumsfeld's Wisdom | Scientific American

https://www.scientificamerican.com/article/rumsfelds-wisdom

5. There are unknown unknowns - Wikipedia

   https://en.wikipedia.org/wiki/There_are_unknown_unknowns

6. Visualizing Connections And Generating New Ideas

   https://fastercapital.com/topics/visualizing-connections-and-generating-new-ideas.html

Publications

1. THE ONE PAGE COMMUNICATOR – It's all about Delivering Clarity – Amazon #1 Best Seller Book (Jul 2023), Golden Book Award 2024
2. THE PROMPTING PLAYBOOK – Fueling Innovations through Generative AI (Oct 2023)
3. THE ONE PAGE COMMUNICATOR – Arabic Edition (Nov 2023)
4. COPORATE CONUNDRUMS & CONFUSIONS – Delivering Clarity. Fueling Efficiency (Dec 2023)
5. BUILD YOUR OWN AI GARAGE (BYOAG) – e-book (March 2024)

"One Page Communicator"

#1 Amazon Best Seller & Golden Book Award 2024

Interaction with other human beings forms the very foundation of society, and throughout the course of history, communication has been pivotal to our evolution. Among the various facets of human behavior that have undergone significant changes during this evolution, one aspect that stands out is communication itself.

In the realm of business, the key to transforming your dreams into success lies in effective communication. The ability to communicate effectively is an esteemed skill, particularly at middle management and senior executive levels.

This book centers around the paramount importance of effective communication within organizations, specifically focusing on the concept of 'One Page Communication' (OPC) and its core components: the audience, message, and purpose. Given the abundance of information across numerous channels and mediums, professionals must strive

to deliver compelling communication that not only fits within a single page but also serves its intended purpose.

Through this book, my objective is to share my experience in creating concise and coherent communication for diverse scenarios across various industry verticals, thereby demonstrating their effectiveness in fulfilling their intended objectives.

I cordially invite you to embark on this journey, as we explore this new era of corporate communication together!

Available in both paperback and Kindle versions across all channels of Amazon globally

Available in both English and Arabic Version

Available in all Amazon channels

amazon amazonkindle

Amazon.in

Amazon.com

"The Prompting Playbook"

Fueling Imagination through Generative AI

Welcome to 'The Prompting Playbook – Fueling Imagination through Generative AI!' by Vasudevan Kidambi, the bestselling author of 'One Page Communicator.' In this comprehensive guide, Vasudevan, renowned for his human-centric problem-solving approach, offers a methodical technique to maximize your interactions with generative AI tools.

In today's world, efficient interaction with AI tools is a necessity, not just for tech enthusiasts but for everyone. This book bridges the gap by providing a systematic approach to crafting prompts that yield precise and meaningful AI generated responses. Whether you're in the corporate world, content creation, or simply curious about generative AI's capabilities, this guide offers practical insights applicable to various scenarios.

With sections covering basic understanding, best practices, formats, and illustrations, each chapter provides real-world examples, and ethical guidelines. Vasudevan's extensive experience in corporate communications and AI tools makes this your 'go-to resource' for mastering the art of effective and responsible interactions with AI tools. Now, you're your imagination with 'The Prompting Playbook.

Available in all Amazon channels

amazon amazonkindle

Amazon.in

Amazon.com

"C3 – Corporate Conundrums & Confusions"

Delivering Clarity, Fueling Efficiency

In the complex and rapidly evolving business landscape, "Corporate Conundrums and Confusions – Delivering Clarity, Fueling Efficiency" emerges as a vital guide for corporate leaders.

This insightful book dissects a range of pressing corporate conundrums and confusions. From the delicate balance between innovation and consistency to unraveling the nuances of Data Lake & Data Warehouse, among many others, each topic is thoroughly explored.

The objective of presenting this book is to help corporate leaders and managers recognize and differentiate between simple terminological confusions and the more profound conundrums that require a fundamentally different approach to resolve effectively.

The insights offered here are not just for the seasoned executives but also for the aspiring younger managers. It's a guide to sharpen their understanding and decision-making skills, helping them avoid common pitfalls and strategic missteps that arise from misinterpretation or a lack of understanding of these critical corporate terminologies.

Through real-life examples and case studies, each term and concept are explained to provide precise meanings. Each conundrum is presented as a set of competing priorities, demanding more than just surface-level understanding. Rather than offering prescriptive solutions, the book delves deep, providing clarity through rich Example(s)s and analyses.

This approach equips leaders with the critical understanding necessary to navigate these challenges effectively. Essential for decision-makers at all levels, this book doesn't just solve problems—it illuminates the path through the intricate maze of modern corporate decision-making. It ensures leaders are well-prepared to tackle any challenge with confidence and strategic acumen.

Available in all Amazon channels

amazon amazonkindle

Amazon.in

Amazon.com

"Build Your Own AI Garage (BYOAG)"

Fuel Your Future with Gen AI

We are unable to imagine modern life without artificial intelligence; it has revolutionized education, communication, and work in our extremely fast digital environment. Generative models stand out above other AI technologies due to their remarkable capacity to generate unique and relevant content across numerous fields.

The goal of this book is to give a thorough examination of the best generative AI tools that are currently available for content generation and curation, image creation and editing, video output, adding voiceover, and getting transcripts, a few of the many areas where AI tools are developed.

Being a published author and a trainer, I know first-hand the struggles that professionals encounter when trying to use new technology to their advantage. If you or your company are interested in using generative AI tools, this book is a great resource. Features, benefits, and limitations of each tool are thoroughly reviewed, along with personal comments derived from my significant experience dealing with these innovative solutions.

The following chapters cover various aspects of generative AI technology where you can discover comprehensive reviews of popular AI tools and their various applications, understand how they are applied in different creative areas, what are their pros and cons, etc. Since I have tested these tools for my research and regular workflow, I have provided my personal review as well to give you a hands-on experience on these tools.

In conclusion, I would like to mention that this book explores deeply into the top generative AI tools available on the market. As a result, you can have a better understanding of these tools and their strengths, weaknesses, and possible uses. By reading this book, you can take advantage of generative AI and keep up with the ever-changing digital scene; you can familiarize yourself with these tools and can incorporate them into your day-to-day operations.

Note: This book is being deliberated as a 'living document' to reflect the continuous changes / updates happening on the AI tools. New information is added, or existing information is revised as and when available to provide the most current and accurate information possible.

www.ingramcontent.com/pod-product-compliance
Lightning Source LLC
LaVergne TN
LVHW041201150826
845673LV00001B/249

* 9 7 8 9 3 6 0 0 6 8 4 8 6 *